Territorial Banking in Nebraska

Territorial Banking in Nebraska

JR Elite Enterprises
2015

by *Leonard M. Owen*

edited by *Jay H. Recher*

Copyright ©2015 by JR Elite Enterprises
All rights reserved. This book or any portion thereof may not be reproduced or used in any manner whatsoever without the express written permission of the publisher except for the use of brief quotations in a book review or scholarly journal.
First Printing: 2015
ISBN: 9780996126403

JR Elite Enterprises
5077 Fruitville Rd Unit 109
Sarasota, Florida 34232
www.NebraskaPaperMoney.com

Ordering Information:
Special discounts are available on quantity purchases by corporations, associations, educators, and others. For details, contact the publisher at the above listed address.
U.S. trade bookstores and wholesalers: Please contact the above listed address

Dedication

To my amazing wife without your continual support this project would never had started let alone finish.

Table of Contents

- Acknowledgements.. viii
- Purpose... ix
- Rarity Scale... x
- Terms Used in This Book.. xi
- Nebraska Banking Overview.. 1
- Bellevue.. 3
  - Fontenelle Bank of Bellevue.. 6
  - Unknown Issuer.. 15
- Brownville... 16
  - Brownville Hotel... 18
  - Nemaha Valley Bank... 22
- Dakota City... 32
  - Bank of Dakota... 34
- De Soto... 38
  - Corn Exchange Bank... 40
  - Bank of De Soto... 49
  - De Soto Bridge & Ferry Company.. 59
  - Waubeek Bank... 60
  - Western Land Exchange Company.. 66
- Florence.. 70
  - Bank of Florence.. 72
- Lincoln... 78
  - Treasurer of the City of Lincoln.. 79
- Nebraska City.. 82
  - McCann & Metcalf... 86
  - Platte Valley Bank.. 87
- Nemaha... 93
  - C.E.L. Holmes.. 94
- Omaha... 99
  - Bank of Nebraska.. 101
  - Brownville Bank & Land Company.. 109
  - City of Omaha.. 114
  - Nebraska Land & Banking Company.. 119
  - Omaha & Chicago Bank.. 123
  - Omaha City Bank & Land Company.. 133
  - Western Exchange & Land Company.. 138

- o Western Exchange, Fire & Marine Insurance Company................................. 143
- Plattsmouth... 157
  - o City of Plattsmouth... 158
- Tekamah... 160
  - o Bank of Tekama in Burt County.. 163
- Appendix A... 169
- Appendix B... 170
- Bibliography... 171

Acknowledgments

The author would like to thank the Central States Numismatic Society for lending the rights to Mr. Owen's book originally written in separate articles and later compiled into one book. A large thank you goes out to those who helped out with scans: The Nebraska State Historical Society, The Durham Museum who holds the Bryon Reed collection, Heritage Auctions, and this book would be no where without the scans and support from James McKee. Last but certainly not least I also want to thank my wife Renae for always giving me positive reinforcement or a kick in the butt when needed.

Purpose

The purpose of this edition is to update a few items from the original text (add color photos), include additional notes mostly in the form of scrip notes; update the rarity of notes and to include a price guide.

Prices will come from a variety of sources: auctions and dealer prices primarily. Not all prices for every grade for every note will be shown. This is for two reasons 1) the condition has yet to be seen 2) no price has yet to be realized at auction or the note has not been be sold in dealer stock. I didn't want to guess what a note would be worth in a given grade. I felt like this would be a disservice to the hobby, and wanted the pricing to be more concise and representative of actual sold notes. These prices will continue to update as more Nebraska notes come to market.

Prepare yourself to pay more than the listed prices for notes graded by a third party (usually PCGS or PMG). Likewise, expect to pay more than UNC prices for notes grading higher than 65 especially those higher than 67.

Most of Mr. Owen's 1984 edition of Territorial Banking in Nebraska will be reprinted here in full. Because Mr. Owen brought such great knowledge to the area of Nebraska territorial banknotes that I have decided to include his vast historical research into each town in this book.

A quick aside regarding the scans used in this book. In some cases it was needed to trim the note to fit on the page - this tactic was mainly used for the sheets with large selvage. This only affected the edges of the note and no note was trimmed where it crossed a significant portion of the border. No scan was touched up in any way to change the look of the note or to make it more attractive. This is unfortunate as a purist, but necessary for spacing.

For more information on Nebraska obsolete paper money please visit: www.NebraskaPaperMoney.com or join the conversation with other collectors at www.facebook.com/nebraskapapermoney

Rarity Scale

R1	Over 200 Notes
R2	101-200
R3	51-100
R4	26-50
R5	11-25
R6	6-10
R7	1-5

This scale is very easy to follow and I've found usually very excepted with collectors. Nebraska obsolete notes will fall into all 'R' numbers. Some banks may be easily found while others are extremely tough.

These 'R' numbers are derived from personal observation, and from other researchers who came before me: Owen, McKee and Walton.

An important note to point out - these 'R' numbers are not concrete and will change over time as notes are found (or lost).

Terms Used in This Book

Altered: The note is genuine but the serial number and/or the signature(s) were added (either contemporary or later). There are some instances that many of the known specimens are altered and are acceptable in the market.

Contemporary Counterfeit: A note that looks like the issued note made to deceive the public during the life of the bank (or shortly thereafter). The purpose was to literally print free money.

Proof: Made in uniface (only the front) usually on India paper (a very thin paper). These were constructed to act as samples either to show the bank to okay designs or for the printer to make sure everything looked as it was supposed to. There was never any intention for proofs to ever circulate. There are on occasion that proof sheets appear and/or proof pairs. Usually someone will cut the sheet in order to make pairs and singles.

Raised: When a genuine note was changed from a lower denomination to a higher denomination. This was done mainly to deceive the public during the life of the bank.

Remainder: If any hand signed area (date, serial number or signature) is missing from the note. If the issued note required two signatures to be valid and the note in question only has one - This would be a remainder regardless of condition.

Spurious: A contemporary attempt to deceive the public by changing the name of the bank. This was often the case with the Waubeek Bank of De Soto.

Nebraska Territory Overview

Most of the early towns in Nebraska were located along the Missouri River, as this was the main source of travel into the area. Many of these towns had their own bank, which issued currency as a medium of exchange, as gold and silver were scarce. A few of these banks ran their business on a sound basis and these banks later became some of the first of the National Banks. Some of the others were in the business to make a fast buck and move on to some other endeavor, leaving the note holders with very little of value.

The following banks received charters from the Territorial Legislature and are known to have issued notes for their banks:

- Western Exchange Fire and Marine Insurance Co., Omaha City, March 16, 1855
- The Bank of Florence, Florence, January 18, 1856
- The Bank of Nebraska, Omaha City, January 18, 1856
- The Nemaha Valley Bank, Brownville, January 18, 1856
- The Platte Valley Bank, Nebraska City, January 18, 1856
- The Fontenelle Bank of Bellevue, Bellevue, January 18, 1856
- The Bank of DeSoto, DeSoto, February 12, 1857
- The Bank of Tekama, Tekamah, February 12, 1857

Note the spelling of the word Tekama (Tekamah). The town of Tekamah spelled its name with an "H" on the end but the spelling of Tekama on the notes was without the "H".

The following banks also issued notes without the benefit of a Territorial Charter:

- The Waubeek Bank, DeSoto
- The Omaha and Chicago Bank, Omaha City
- The Bank of Dakota, Dakota City
- The Corn Exchange Bank, DeSoto
- The Omaha City Bank and Land Co., Omaha City
- The Brownville Bank and Land Co., (Supposedly to have been in Omaha City, but actually never had offices there).
- The Nebraska Land and Banking Co., Omaha City
- The Western Land and Exchange Co., DeSoto
- The Western Exchange and Land Co., Omaha City

Only two of these banks are recorded in early history books as being of sound character. The Bank of Dakota, located in Dakota City, which operated without a Territorial Charter, and the Platte Valley Bank of Nebraska City, which had a Territorial Charter.

Bellevue

Bellevue is mentioned in the Centennial Gazetteer of 1874 in the following manner: "A postal village and the county seat of Sarpy County, Nebraska, near the Missouri River, 15 miles south of Omaha and 18 miles north of Plattsmouth. On the spot where the village now stands, the famous explorers Lewis and Clark landed in 1804, and soon afterward the American Fur Company established a trading post here."

This information would indicate that Bellevue has the distinction of being the first white settlement in the territory that was later to become the State of Nebraska. The early history books of Douglas County and of Nebraska do not agree on this issue. A.T. Andreas' "History of the State of Nebraska" says that Sarpy County contains the oldest settlement in the State. This settlement is Bellevue. Sarpy County was organized on February 1, 1857. Prior to this time, the land in Sarpy County, as well as the town of Bellevue, was a part of Douglas County.

The following is from Mr. Andreas's history: "Lewis and Clark, in their famous expedition in search of the head-waters of the Missouri, reached the mouth of the Platte River on July 21, 1804, and the next day explored the country to the north and west, and camped on the level bench on which Bellevue was half a century later located.

The following year, Manuel Lesa (Lisa), a Spanish adventurer, came to Bellevue, and on climbing the bluff to the plateau, was, as the story goes, so struck with the natural beauty of the spot, that he exclaimed "Bellevue", and unwittingly christened the town.

It is probable that other parties visited the junction of the two great rivers between the date given and 1810, but if such was the case, they have left no record. In 1810, the American Fur Company, which was always in the van of civilization, established a trading post at this point, and placed Francis Deroin in charge as Indian trader. Mr. Deroin was succeeded by Joseph Roubideaux, familiarly known as "Old Joe" to all the settlers, and later the father of St. Joseph, Missouri. In 1816, John Carbanne succeeded Roubideaux and held the position until superseded in 1824 by Col. Peter A. Sarpy."

Mr. Andres' history, written in 1882, as well as some of the other early historians, tends to agree with the above version of the founding of Bellevue.

Addison E. Sheldon, in his history, "Nebraska, The Land and the People," as well as other historians, says that Fort Atkinson was the "First White Settlement in Nebraska." Since this writer did not arrive in Nebraska until about 130 years after this part of Nebraska history was written, the correct version is left to the reader's choice.

Regardless of the above controversy, Bellevue was a very early settlement in the Territory of Nebraska and was a prime contender for the first Territorial Capitol which was established in Omaha City.

In 1823, the Indian agency that had previously been established at Fort Atkinson was removed to Bellevue and was known in government reports as the "Council Bluffs Indian Agency at Bellevue."

In 1846, the Presbyterian Board of Missions selected the Rev. Edward McKinney to establish a post as a suitable site. He selected Bellevue as the site. A building to house the post was completed in 1848.

Mr. Andreas stats that, "In 1852, Maj. Barrow, Col. Stephen Decatur and others conceived the idea of laying out a town, but it was not until February 9, 1854, that a company was organized for that purpose, and the agreement signed by the following persons: Peter Sarpy, Stephen Decatur, Hiram Bennett, Isaiah N. Bennett, George Nepner, William R. English, James M. Galeswood, George T. Turner, P.J. McMahon, A.W. Hollister, and A.C. Ford, who were the original proprietors of the town, and were known as the "Old Town Company."

But there were no settlements in the West at that date to support a town, and the city proved to be an elephant on the hands of the incorporators. Most of the land owned by the company passed into other hands, and the company itself dissolved by the process of natural decay."

The Indian title to the lands in and around Bellevue ended in July, 1854, by treaty between the Indians and the government. This treaty opened up the lands for the settlement of pioneers. Bellevue did not grow to any great extent until 1857. Col. Benton established a steam ferry at this point and Bellevue, as well as Sarpy County, began to grow.

As was stated earlier, the Bellevue Town Company was organized in 1854. In 1856, the Fontenelle Bank of Bellevue opened for business and closed its door for the last time in the fall of the following year. Bellevue was organized as a city in 1856 with a full set of city officials. The first mayor was Reuben Lovejoy. He was followed by George Jennings. Others held this post until the election of Stephen D. Bangs in 1873. Mr. Bangs was re-elected in 1874. The elections were dropped at this point in time, which left Mr. Bangs as a perpetual incumbent, as the mayor of a defunct city. The county seat was transferred to Papillion in 1876, which further reflected Bellevue's decline.

Bellevue has one bank known as the "Fontenelle Bank of Bellevue." This bank received its charter from the second Territorial Legislature on January 18, 1856. This corporation was formed by the following men: John B. Sarpy, Peter A. Sarpy, Samuel Knepper,

John R. Cecil, Lathrup B. Kinney, Phillip J. McMahon, Leavitt L. Brown, and John Clancy. This bank received 1 25-year charter and was to go into business when $50,000 had been subscribed.

The Nebraska City News made the following statement on June 12, 1858: "The Fontenelle Bank of Bellevue was chartered at the legislative session of 1855-1856, the principal figure and manager to secure its incorporation being General L.L. Bowen of that place, who probably realized about $3,000 by sale of the same to Greene, Weare, and Company. This bank failed last fall, benefiting the bill holders by swindling them out of $150,000 and thereby illustrating the fact that 'Corporations have no souls,' and that some banks have no bodies."

All signed notes known to exist from this bank were signed by John Weare as president and John J. Town as cashier, with a variety of dates.

These notes circulated from the banks of Greene and Weare in the following Iowa towns: Cedar Rapids, Des Moines, Marion, Vinton, Osage, Council Bluffs, Fort Dodge, and Sioux City.

Notes from this bank are known in the following denominations: $1 (plate position A), $1 (pp B), $2 (pp A), $3 (pp A), $5 (pp A), $5 (pp B), $5 (pp C), and $10 (pp A).

The lament of the 'Nebraska City News' seems to have been a bit harsh when we look at the scarcity of these notes today. Both cancelled and uncancelled notes of this bank are obtainable but the uncancelled notes are scarcer.

We also see that the history books had Bellevue about ready to dry up and blow away in the mid-1870's, which did not happen, as was the fate of some of the other early Nebraska towns. Bellevue today is still on the map and is a thriving community of about 52,000 people as of 2012.

All notes from this bank were printed by Danforth, Wright and Company.

Fontenelle Bank of Bellevue: Nebraska's Oldest Commercial Building

When the Nebraska territory formed in 1854 banks were on the top of the legislature's thoughts when they defined the first criminal code which specifically stated that "participating in any form of banking [is punishable] by imprisonment in the county jail not exceeding one year or by a fine of not less than $1,000." At the same time banking proved to be a necessity if any economy outside of a simple barter system was to exist. Thus the first corporation granted in Nebraska was to the Western Fire & Marine Insurance Co. of Omaha, purely a sham bank whose only right was to "receive deposits and issue certificates thereof."

A few months after the "insurance company" was chartered, in December of 1855, Peter Sarpy of Bellevue, General L. L. Bowen of Elgin, Illinois and six other men applied for a banking charter from the territorial legislature. Their Fontenelle Bank of Bellevue was one of 12 banking applicants entered on the same date. Over the strong objections of J. Sterling Morton, their bank, and those of four others were granted charters.

In 1856 a two-story building of handmade bricks was completed on the northwest corner of Mission and Main Streets. The Transitional Greek Revival-Italianate rectangular building faced Main Street with an exterior staircase leading to the second floor on the northwest corner of the structure, facing west. The banking rooms and vault were on the first floor.

The bank's actual 25 year charter was dated January 18, 1856, allowed up to $500,000 of capital stock and was permitted to open as soon as $50,000 had been subscribed and paid in. Before the bank had been in existence a year it was sold to Greene, Ware & Co. of Cedar Rapids, Iowa with General Bowen personally profiting $3,000. Almost at once Greene & Ware commenced printing notes on the bank in the denominations of $1, $2, $3, $5 and $10 all of which, including the $3 bills were fairly common in the period. Because the notes were not secured by gold or silver, they circulated only so long as public confidence in the bank existed. Unfortunately their timing left a great deal to be desired as 1857 proved to be a year of nation-wide depression. Sadly the Fontenelle Bank of Bellevue and virtually all of the territory's fledgling financial institutions failed within months. Banking historian A. G. Warner was quick to point out that the bank was not to be considered a home-owned institution but the result was the same. Reports of the amount of outstanding banknotes varied from $35,000 as reported by the Dakota City Herald on September 10, 1859 to $150,000 noted in the Nebraska City News June 12, 1858. The Nebraska City paper also stated that this and other bank failures were proof that "corporations have no souls."

It is an ill wind that blows no good however and just as the bank failure occurred, the territorial legislature created Sarpy County to correct an inequity in representation. With the new county seat located in Bellevue, the bank building proved an excellent courthouse with the upstairs converted to a courtroom. On January 30, 1861 Sarpy County purchased the old bank building and two adjacent lots for $1,500. Interestingly the committee in charge of the sale was headed by General Bowen. As county courthouse the upper floor was also used as a meeting room, dance hall and opera house.

An election in 1875 relocated the Sarpy County seat to Papillion allowing the county to rent the bank courthouse to Bellevue for use as a city hall. 50 years later, in 1925, the city bought the building for $600. In 1959 Bellevue built a new city hall and it looked as if the old building would be razed. In order to save the structure, Mrs. Harold LeMar bought it the following year for $10,000 and rented it out to a variety of retail shops. The City of Bellevue realized it had allowed a historic relic to slip away and repurchased the building in 1972 for its appraised value of $36,000.

Without a vast expenditure, the building was restored around the extant vault as its original use as a bank. Today what is undoubtedly the oldest commercial structure in Nebraska is on the National Register of Historic Buildings, looking almost exactly as it did in 1856, the only minor alterations being a new roof line and front steps.

Uncancelled notes are scarce thus command a higher premium. All notes will have the signatures of John Ware as President and John J. Town as Cashier.

Bellevue – The Fontenelle Bank of Bellevue

Fate: Failed
Date: 1856

Jim McKee Collection

Owen Number	Denomination	Plate Position(s)	Basic Info.	Cross Refs.	Rarity
1-1	$1	A-B	Protector: Large ONE in Red Imprint: Danforth, Wright and Co.	Haxby: 5G2a Walton: 1 McKee: 1	R.4

	G	VG	F	VF
Cancelled	-	$50	$70	-
Uncancelled	$100	$125	$140	$200
Proof	-	-	-	-

Patrick K Millike Collection

Owen Number	Denomination	Plate Position(s)	Basic Info.	Cross Refs.	Rarity
1-2	$2	A	Protector: Large TWO in Red Imprint: Danforth, Wright and Co.	Haxby: 5G4a Walton: 2 McKee: 2	R.4

	G	VG	F	VF
Cancelled	$50	-	$125	-
Uncancelled	$60	$75	-	-
Proof	-	-	-	-

Patrick K Millike Collection

Owen Number	Denomination	Plate Position(s)	Basic Info.	Cross Refs.	Rarity
1-3	$3	A	Protector: Large THREE in Red Imprint: Danforth, Wright and Co.	Haxby: 5G6a Walton: 3 McKee: 3	R.4

	G	VG	F	VF
Cancelled	-	$80	$125	-
Uncancelled	-	$100	$130	-
Proof	-	-	-	-

10

Patrick K Millike Collection

Owen Number	Denomination	Plate Position(s)	Basic Info.	Cross Refs.	Rarity
1-4	$5	A-C	Protector: Large 5 in Red Imprint: Danforth, Wright and Co.	Haxby: 5G8a Walton: 4 McKee: 4	R.4

	VG	F	VF	UNC
Cancelled	-	$110	-	-
Uncancelled	$75	$130	-	-
Proof*	-	-	-	$700

* Three are know from the Christie's "Elizabeth" sale in 1990.

Patrick K Millike Collection

Owen Number	Denomination	Plate Position(s)	Basic Info.	Cross Refs.	Rarity
1-5	$10	A	Protector: Large TEN in Red	Haxby: 5G10a	R.5
				Walton: 5	
			Imprint: Danforth, Wright and Co.	McKee: 5	

	G	VG	F	VF
Cancelled	-	$60	$85	-
Uncancelled	-	-	-	-
Proof	-	-	-	-

Image Courtesy of Heritage Auctions.

Owen Number	Denomination	Plate Position(s)	Basic Info.	Cross Refs.	Rarity
1-6	$1-$1-$2-$3	A-B	Protector: None	Haxby: N/A	R.7
			Imprint: Danforth, Wright and Co.	Walton: N/A	
				McKee: N/A	

	F	XF	AU	UNC
Proof Sheet*	-	-	-	$3,220

* This type sold at the Christie's Sale in 1990 along with a $5-$5-$5-$10 sheet for $1,450.

13

Image Courtesy of Heritage Auctions.

Owen Number	Denomination	Plate Position(s)	Basic Info.	Cross Refs.	Rarity
1-7	$5-$5-$5-$10	A-C	Protector: Large VALUE in Red	Haxby: N/A	R.7
				Walton: N/A	
			Imprint: Danforth, Wright and Co.	McKee: N/A	

	F	XF	AU	UNC
Sheet*	-	-	$3,000	-

* This type sold at the Christie's Sale in 1990 along with a $1-$1-$2-$3 sheet for $1,450.

Bellevue – Unknown Issuer

Fate: Unknown
Date: 1857-69 (based on when the printer was in business)

Image Courtesy of Heritage Auctions.

Owen Number	Denomination	Plate Position(s)	Basic Info.	Cross Refs.	Rarity
2-1	$1	N/A	Protector: Large ONE in Gray Imprint: P.S. Duval & Son	Haxby: N/A Walton: N/A McKee: N/A	R.7
	VG	VF	XF	AU	
Remainder	-	$825	-	-	

* Little is known about this issuer except that it's a post note, and that it was printed sometime between 1857 and 1869 which is solely based on when the printer was "P.S. Duval & Son". This coincides with when Nebraska was still a territory.
** Currently there is only one note know it's graded by PCGS Very Fine 25 apparent for rust, damage, and mounting remnants on the back. It was last sold by Heritage Auctions in April 2013.

Brownville

The town of Brownville, Nebraska was named after Richard Brown, who arrived in Brownville on August 29, 1854. Mr. Brown lived in Brownville for several years before moving to Texas. Thomas B. Edwards and his wife arrived a few weeks later and Mrs. Edwards was reported to be the first white woman to live in Brownville.

Taulbird Edwards built the first permanent building in the town and the first white child to be born was the daughter of Mr. and Mrs. John Fitzgerald, who was born October 20, 1854. Samuel Stiers and Nancy Swift were married by Rev. Joel M. Wood in October, 1854, and gained the distinction of being the first couple to be married at Brownville.

H.S. Thorpe was the first school teacher, who held school in a log cabin near Main Street. This cabin was also used for the first District Court to hold their meetings. The first frame school building was erected in 1856 and was later used as a home.

The first general store was opened by William Hoblitzell and Isaac T. Whyte in March, 1855. Crance & McCallister opened the second general store in 1857. Crane & McCallister were suppliers of merchandise for Denver and other points west. J.C. Deuser was the first tinsmith to open shop in Brownville and Williams T. Den was the first shoemaker. The first steam mill was started by Henry and Jerome Hoover and was completed by Richard Brown, Samuel Rogers, and Henry Emerson in 1855. Richard Brown was one of the original incorporators of the Nemaha Valley Bank of Brownville and Samuel Rogers became a part owner of this bank on March 18, 1857.

Joel M. Wood built the first hotel in Brownville on Main Street in 1855, and Dr. A.S. Holladay arrived in November, 1855, to become the first physician and druggist. Daniel L. McGary arrived in February, 1856, to become the first lawyer, and Richard Brown was the first postmaster.

Mr. A.T. Andreas, in his "History of the State of Nebraska," published in 1882, made the following statements for the period of 1857 and 1858: "The following picture of Brownville a quarter of a century ago, when between 40 and 50 steamers were plying regularly in the Missouri River trade, is painted by an early settler. The boundaries of Brownville were mostly between Atlantic and College streets and between Second and the river."

To show the importance attained by Brownville as a business point within the two years after the arrival of Richard Brown, in 1854 the first issue of the first newspaper (The Advertiser of June 7, 1856) claims that the village contained at that date two dry goods and grocery stores, a schoolhouse, church, courthouse, steam saw mill, lath and shingle machine, cabinet shop, two blacksmith shops, one banking house, one hotel, several boarding houses, and a population of 400 persons.

In the early days, and under the position that a Southern man had as much right to take his slaves to the Territories as a Northern man had to carry his horses or cattle with him, several slaves were brought to Brownville. Richard Brown, founder of the town, brought one from Holt County, Missouri, and Col. G.H. Nixon, first Registrar of the Land Office, was the proprietor of two or three slaves that were brought from his old home in Tennessee. Col. Nixon was a strong pro-slavery man, and on the breaking out of the rebellion, he went south and fought for his own side.

At the close of the war, he met one of his former slaves who were engaged in teaching a colored school. The Colonel greeted him heartily and said to him, "You are not qualified to teach your people, but I want to help you, and will see that you have an education." After a thorough common school course, the former slave again went south, and is now at the head of a Southern seminary for the education of colored children. Thus, it will be seen that the early settlers of Otoe County are mistaken in the supposition there were no slaves in any other county but their own.

The Brownville Hotel Company

The Brownville Hotel Company was formed on June 27, 1857 with the sole purpose to construct the best hotel in the area. This company was comprised of James W. Coleman, Alexander Hallam, C. W. Wheeler, H. Johnson, and R. Brown, as Directors. These in their turn elected C. W. Wheeler, President; and Alexander Hallam, Secretary and Treasurer. The location of the hotel was on 2nd and Main Streets and was fifty by eighty feet and three stories high. In October of the same year this group decided to issue scrip to found the completion of the hotel. The notes were going to be payable one year after the date, bearing 20% interest. $6,000 worth of scrip was printed and $5,951 were redeemed and later destroyed. The hotel was finished in the spring of 1858.

This leaves $49 left for collectors. In Walton's book he mentions that the NSHS has one $5, three $2s, and two $1s. From the records list that this researcher came across the NSHS has one $5, four $2s and two $1s. Either there is only $36 or $34 leftover. It is unknown if the NSHS notes are from runoff or apart of the $49. Like most other Nebraska scrip notes these are very rare and hard to come by. All notes that have been seen have "cancelled" written in pen.

The man named on the note, John McPherson was a Brownville citizen. He moved into town in 1855 after practicing medicine in Ohio. It isn't all that clear why he is named on the note, but it may be fair to guess that he had large sums of capitol and enjoyed being a 19th century entrepreneur. He was a doctor, owned a mercantile store, flour and saw mill, a cigar manufacturing plant and later in 1872 moved his affairs to Republican City some 200 miles west. Also, Dr. McPherson had a controlling interest in the Brownville Hotel at some point throughout 1859-1870.

At the time of this printing the only auction/dealer pricing that could be found was for the $1. It would seem that if a $2 or $5 came to the auction block in XF expect to pay at least the same as the listed price maybe more since these hardly are sold in public forums.

Brownville – The Brownville Hotel Company

Fate: Property Completed
Date: 1857

NSHS Collection

Owen Number	Denomination	Plate Position(s)	Basic Info.	Cross Refs.	Rarity
3-1	$1	A	Protector: None	Haxby: N/A	R.7
			Imprint: Furnas & Langdon Print	Walton: 1	
				McKee: 1	

	VF	XF	AU	UNC
Pen Cancelled	-	$1,000	-	-

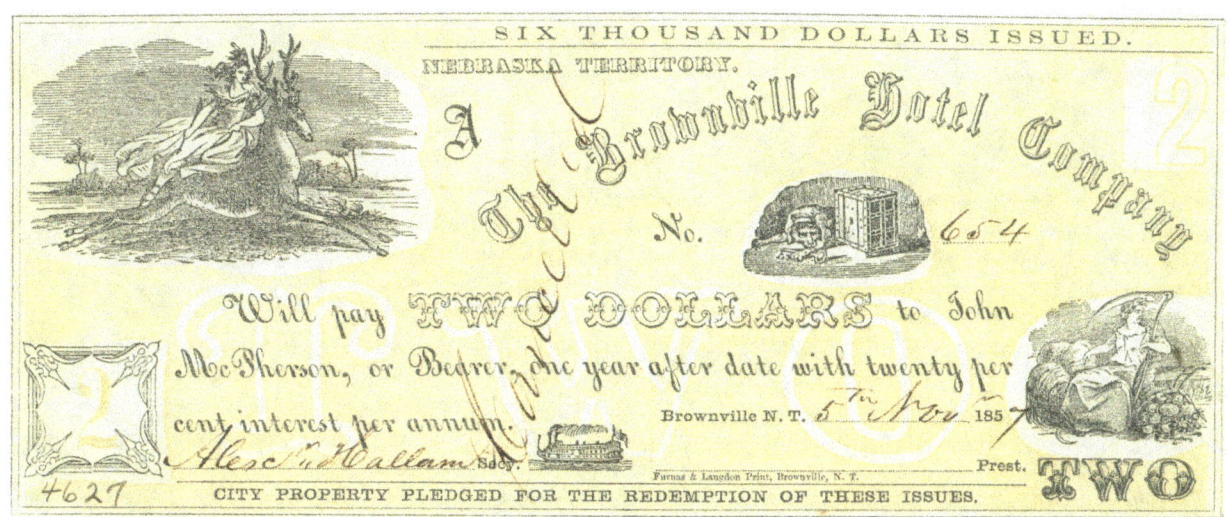

NSHS Collection

Owen Number	Denomination	Plate Position(s)	Basic Info.	Cross Refs.	Rarity
3-2	$2	A	Protector: Large TWO in White Imprint: Furnas & Langdon Print	Haxby: N/A Walton: 2 McKee: 2	R.7

	VF	XF	AU	UNC
Pen Cancelled	-	-	-	-

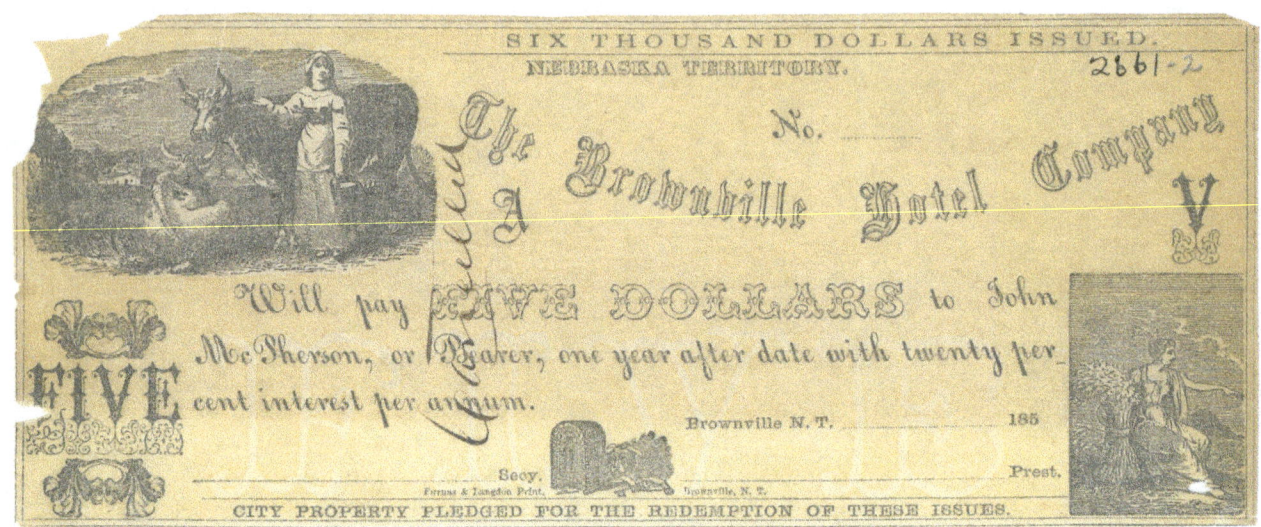

NSHS Collection

Owen Number	Denomination	Plate Position(s)	Basic Info.	Cross Refs.	Rarity
3-3	$5	A	Protector: Large FIVE in White Imprint: Furnas & Langdon Print	Haxby: N/A Walton: 3 McKee: 2	R.7

	VF	XF	AU	UNC
Pen Cancelled Remainder	-	-	-	-

Nemaha Valley Bank

The Nemaha Valley Bank of Brownville received its charter from the Territorial Legislature on January 18, 1856. The original incorporators of this bank were Clement Brown, James S. Brown, Benjamin B. Frazier, Volney Brown, Richard M. Waterman, and Richard Brown. This was the usual charter with the capital stock of $50,000 and the authorization to print and distribute bank notes, bonds, and certificates of indebtedness.

The following men joined the management of the Nemaha Valley Bank in July of 1856: Samuel H. Riddle, Henn (this may have been Berhart Henn, who was a member of Congress in Washington in 1854 from the Iowa District, as all of the other new members of management team from this bank were from Council bluffs, Iowa), Williams & Company, and Benjamin R. Pegram. With the change of management, contracts were entered into for the construction of a new two-story brick building to be erected at the corner of Main and Second streets. This was the location of the bank after the completion of the building in the fall of 1857.

The management was again changed on March 18, 1857, when Samuel H. Riddle and Benjamin R. Pegram sold their interests in the bank to Jones, Barkalow, Rogers, Davidson and Associates. The bank again changed management in July, 1857 when T.L. Mackoy of Galesburg, Illinois became the President of the institution.

Mr. Mackoy announced that notes of this bank would be redeemed at current rates in Brownville, by E.J. Tinkham and Co., Bankers, Chicago; John J. Anderson and Co., Bankers, St. Louis; Warren County Bank, Monmouth, Illinois; and T.L. Mackoy and Co., Bankers, Galesburg, Illinois.

This bank suspended payment of its obligations in September, 1857, because of the panic in money matters throughout the country. The bank started to again redeem their notes in November, 1857, but when the District Court decided that their charter had been violated, the redemption was stopped, and J.L. Carson, O.B. Hewett, and J.S. Minick were appointed trustees to wind up the affairs of the bank.

This bank probably changed hand more times than any other bank in the state of Nebraska, and at the time of its failure, the bank was under the management of its cashier, Alexander Hallam.

Two different types of notes were printed for this bank, with the first type being printed by Wellstood, Hay and Whiting. This type is known in the denominations of $1 and $2. The second type was printed by Toppan, Carpenter, and Co. This type is known in the denominations of $1, $2, $3, $5 and $10.

With all the changes in the management of this institution, the collector of these notes will be able to find several different signature combinations to look for, as well as looking for the various types and denominations.

Haxby lists the Lazy 1 (Owen 4-1) and the Lazy 2 (Owen 4-3) as remainders. It's fair to assume that since the bank went through many different owners and thus signers that these two notes stock could have been transferred from one owner to the next. It's again fair to assume that all of these lazy notes never were intended to reach the populous of Brownville - this would create altered notes in order to further deceive contemporaneously. Either way these notes are rare and collectible in any condition.

For the purpose of this book these lazy notes that are signed, dated and have serial numbers will be considered issued, and those with one or more of the aforementioned missing will be considered a remainder, and not altered.

There are two denominations that are known to have proofs (4-3, 4-4 and 4-7) there are fewer than 5 known of each. The $1 (4-2) and the $5 (4-6) proofs were added to keep some consistency between this reference and Haxby's. I was not able to find any other scans (besides of the $1 in Haxby) or any realized pricing at auction. The prices are in line with other final auction values of other denominations in the conditions listed. However, at this time no proof sheets are known to exist.

Owen 4-2, 4-4, 4-6, and 4-7 have been seen with a purple stamp "Not United States currency has no value" this is often times stamped more than once.

Brownville – The Nemaha Valley Bank

Fate: Failed
Date: 1856-58

Jim McKee Collection

Owen Number	Denomination	Plate Position(s)	Basic Info.	Cross Refs.	Rarity
4-1	$1	A-B	Protector: Large Lazy ONE in Red Imprint: Wellstood, Hay & Whiting	Haxby: 10G4a Walton: 1 McKee: 2	R.6

	VG	F	VF	XF
Issued	-	$950	$1500	-
Remainder	$330	-	$725	-

Owen Number	Denomination	Plate Position(s)	Basic Info.	Cross Refs.	Rarity
4-2	$1	A	Protector: Large ONE in Red Imprint: Toppan, Carpenter & Co.	Haxby: 10G2a Walton: 3 McKee: 1	R.2

	VG	F	VF	XF
Issued	$85	$100	$175	-
With Purple Stamp	-	$115	-	-
Proof	-	-	-	$900

25

Owen Number	Denomination	Plate Position(s)	Basic Info.	Cross Refs.	Rarity
4-3	$2	A	Protector: Large Lazy TWO in Red Imprint: Wellstood, Hay & Whiting	Haxby: 10G8a Walton: 2 McKee: 4	R.6

	VG	F	VF	XF
Issued	-	$600	-	-
Remainder	$725	$800	$975	-
Proof	-	-	-	$900

Byron Reed Collection

Owen Number	Denomination	Plate Position(s)	Basic Info.	Cross Refs.	Rarity
4-4	$2	A	Protector: Large TWO in Red Imprint: Toppan, Carpenter & Co.	Haxby: 10G6a Walton: 4 McKee: 3	R.2

	VG	F	VF	UNC
Issued	$65	$90	-	-
Remainder	$25	-	-	-
With Purple Stamp	-	$80	$120	-
Proof	-	-	-	$1500

NSHS Collection

Owen Number	Denomination	Plate Position(s)	Basic Info.	Cross Refs.	Rarity
4-5	$3	A	Protector: Large 3 in Red	Haxby: 10G10a	R.7
			Imprint: Toppan, Carpenter & Co.	Walton: 5	
				McKee: 5	

	VF	XF	AU	UNC
Remainder	$1000	$1200	-	-

Owen Number	Denomination	Plate Position(s)	Basic Info.	Cross Refs.	Rarity
4-6	$5	A	Protector: Large V in Red	Haxby: 10G12a	R.2
			Imprint: Toppan, Carpenter & Co.	Walton: 6	
				McKee: 6	

	F	VF	XF	AU
Issued	$70	$190	-	-
Remainder	-	$100	-	-
With Purple Stamp	$80	-	$120	-
Proof	-	-	-	$1000

Owen Number	Denomination	Plate Position(s)	Basic Info.	Cross Refs.	Rarity
4-7	$10	A	Protector: Large TEN in Red	Haxby: 10G16a	R.3
			Imprint: Toppan, Carpenter & Co.	Walton: 7	
				McKee: 7	

	F	VF	XF	AU
Issued	$100	$160	-	-
With Purple Stamp	$230	-	-	-
Proof	-	-	-	$1050

Image Courtesy of Heritage Auctions.

Owen Number	Denomination	Plate Position(s)	Basic Info.	Cross Refs.	Rarity
4-8	$1-$2-$5-$3	A	Protector: Large VALUE in Red	Haxby: N/A	R.7
				Walton: N/A	
			Imprint: Toppan, Carpenter & Co.	McKee: N/A	

	F	VF	XF	AU
Sheet	$2000	$2300	-	-

Dakota City

The Bank of Dakota City was owned by Augustus Kountze. The notes from this bank are very scarce as Mr. Kountze only allowed $3,000 of his issue to be in circulation at any one time and these notes were redeemed on presentation. After closing his bank in Dakota City, Mr. Kountze moved to Omaha City and opened a bank with his brothers, Herman, Luther, Charles and William. This bank was merged with the First National Bank of Omaha in July 1865.

Augustus Kountze served in the following capacities at various times: The owner of a bank, Director of The First National Bank, Territorial Treasurer, State Treasurer, and incorporator of the Union Pacific Railroad, Director of the Union Pacific Railroad, incorporator of the Omaha and Northwestern Railroad, Director of the Omaha and Northwestern Railroad, member of the Dakota Company, partner in the building of the Grand Central Hotel, incorporator of the Omaha Horse Railway Co., and many other posts.

William F. Lockwood was the President of the Bank of Dakota City and James W. Virtue was the Cashier. Most of the signed notes from this bank were signed by these two men, Mr. Lockwood was a Territorial Judge and Mr. Virtue was appointed as the first Postmaster of Dakota City. However, at least one note (an Owen 5-1) is known with the signature of Augustus Kountze as cashier with the serial number 2799 and plate position B. This note has been severely circulated missing approximately one-third of the note.

Dakota County was created by the first Territorial Legislature on March 7, 1855. Dakota City was made the County Seat of Dakota County by an act of the Territorial Legislature on January 23, 1856. Some of the people desired a more central location for the County Seat. St. Johns was to be the new location. A vote was taken on August 2, 1858. The County Seat remained in Dakota City.

A preliminary survey of Dakota City was made in 1855. In September of 1856 it was surveyed under the direction of the Dakota City Company, of which Augustus Kountze was President. The first building erected in Dakota City was built by B.F. Chambers in May of 1856. It was a log cabin with a flat roof of dirt and a dirt floor. This building was later improved and enlarged by Dr. J.D.M. Crockwell and was occupied as a hotel under the name of the "Chihuahua House". Dakota City had hopes of becoming a metropolis in the early days, and through the influence of Dr. Crockwell, the United States Land Office was established here in 1857. A Large three-story hotel with a two-story wing was built in Dakota City at a cost of $16,000 in gold.

The United States Court was held here twice a year, in the spring and fall. Abraham Lincoln, in 1861, appointed William F. Lockwood as Judge of the Third Judicial District of the Territory.

With the admission of Nebraska as a State, however, the prospects for Dakota City changed. The United States Court no longer held semi-annual meetings here. The business of the Land Office diminished, and in September of 1875 it was moved to Niobrara. With the decline of this business, the Grand Central Hotel was no longer needed. In 1979, it was torn down and sold as old lumber. A two-story brick school house was built in 1866 at a cost of $4,500.

The Centennial "Gazetteer" of the United States, printed in 1874, has this to say about Dakota City, Nebraska: "Dakota City is a postal village and the county seat of Dakota County, Nebraska. It is six miles southwest of Sioux City Iowa, and has a population of 300. It was considerable local trade, and manufacturers, and one local newspaper."

Dakota City is in the Northeast part of Nebraska with a population of 1,919 as of the 2010 Census (a population of 819 in 1860). It is bordered on the northeast and east by the Missouri River, which separates it from Dakota and Iowa. The terrain consists of rolling prairies with well timbered bottom lands along streams. The bottoms are very productive, while the uplands are excellent for grazing purposes. Dakota City still remains the County Seat today.

The price differences between issued and remainder are inconsequential as these notes are rare in any grade or type with fewer than 5 notes being known for each of the denominations.

Dakota City – The Bank of Dakota

Fate: Moved to Omaha and became the First National Bank of Nebraska
Date: ca. 1858-60

Byron Reed Collection

Owen Numbert	Denomination	Plate Position(s)	Basic Info.	Cross Refs.	Rarity
5-1	$1	A-B	Protector: 1 in Red	Haxby: 15G2a	R.7
			Imprint: Danforth, Wright & Co.	Walton: 1	
				McKee: 1	

	AG	VG	Fine	VF
Issued	-	$800	-	-
Remainder	$400	-	$1500	$2000

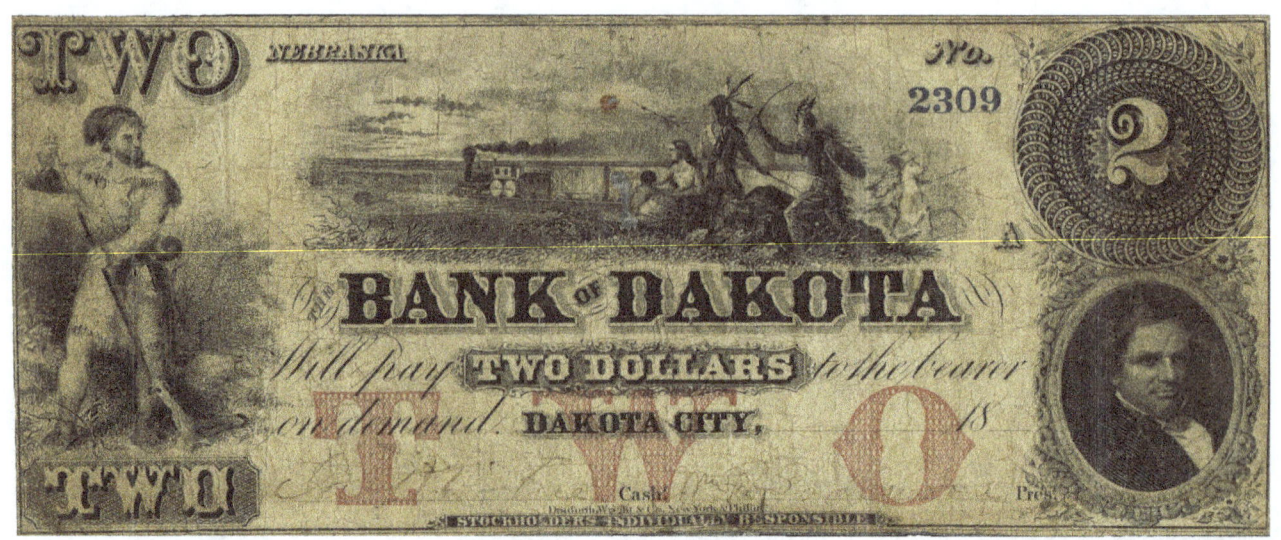

Image Courtesy of Heritage Auctions.

Owen Number	Denomination	Plate Position(s)	Basic Info.	Cross Refs.	Rarity
5-2	$2	A	Protector: Large TWO in Red Imprint: Danforth, Wright & Co.	Haxby: 15G4a Walton: 2 McKee: 2	R.7

	G	VG	Fine	VF
Issued	-	-	-	-
Remainder	$950	-	-	-

Image Courtesy of Heritage Auctions.

Owen Number	Denomination	Plate Position(s)	Basic Info.	Cross Refs.	Rarity
5-3	$5	A	Protector: Large FIVE in Red Imprint: Danforth, Wright & Co.	Haxby: 15G6a Walton: 3 McKee: 3	R.7

	G	VG	Fine	VF
Issued	-	-	-	-
Remainder	-	-	$700	$1,100

Image Courtesy of Heritage Auctions.

Owen Number	Denomination	Plate Position(s)	Basic Info.	Cross Refs.	Rarity
5-4	$1-$1-$2-$5	A	Protector: Large VALUE in Red	Haxby: N/A*	R.7
				Walton: N/A	
			Imprint: Danforth, Wright & Co.	McKee: N/A	

	G	VG	Fine	VF
Remainder	-	-	-	$5,500**

*Haxby had the wrong sheet configuration ($1-$2-$5-$5) and is listed as 15X1.
**This sheet was sold during the ABN Sale at Christie's in 1990 for $2,200
***The image on the right is of the steel plate that was sold 7/27/08 by Stack's for $6,612.50.

De Soto

The "Gazetter" of 1874 mad the following statement about De Soto: De Soto, postal village in Washington County, Nebraska, on the Missouri River, and the Omaha & Northwestern Railroad, 26 miles from Omaha. This is a very brief notation of a town that was a thriving community a few short years prior to 1874. The town of De Soto was platted in 1854 and was incorporated on March 7, 1855.

The following information is to be found in the History of Nebraska by A.T. Andreas, written in 1862: "De Soto is situated about four miles southeast of Blair, on the Missouri River, and on the Chicago, St. Paul, Minneapolis, and Omaha Railroad. The town was laid out in the fall of 1857 by Dr. John Glover, Gen. J.B. Robinson, Potter C. Sullivan, E.P. Scott, William Clancy, and others, but no actual settlement was made until the following spring."

On March 7, 1885, the town was incorporated, and in the summer of that year thirty hewn log houses were built. The first store was opened by Dr. A. Phinney; the first postmaster was Potter C. Sullivan; and the first mercantile firm was that of Kennard Brothers, established in 1856. Judge Jesse T. Davis, now a resident of Blair, was one of the early settlers.

By 1857 De Soto was a thriving community of about 700 people that could boast a banking metropolis with three banks. These banks were The Bank of De Soto, The Waubeek Bank, and The Western Land and Exchange Co. Records indicate that the Western Land and Exchange Co. became the Corn Exchange Bank in the summer of 1860. A proof $1 note from the Western Land and Exchange Co. is known to exist but no known specimen of circulation notes has surfaced.

De Soto was the county seat of Washington County from 1858-1866. In 1978 the last building was torn down (the De Soto Store) and currently the only thing left is a farm in which three families reside.

The Bank of De Soto received its charter from the Third Territorial Legislature by an override of the veto of Governor Mark W. Izard. This charter was secured by P.J. McMahon, W.D. Brown, Paul Jones, J.W. Bristol, and James Jones. All of these men had Wisconsin interests. This was the usual 25 year charter and it was granted on February 12, 1857. This bank changed hands several times and "went bust" in the spring of 1862. Its last issue, dated October 1, 1863, arrived after the bank had closed so these notes were never put into circulation. These notes are among the more common of the Nebraska notes today.

However, according to "Banker's Almanac 1861" this bank had $100,000 in capital and still had an undisclosed amount of notes in circulation. Including Bank of Florence (Owen 11), Platte Valley Bank (Owen 13), Bank of Nebraska (Owen 15), Bank of Tekama (Owen 22), and Western Marine Insurance Co. (Owen 24) there were a total of $600,000 in circulation and the banks retained $100,000 in specie in 1861. The bank operated for another couple of years after this report. The notes in circulation that would have been reported would be Owen 7-1 through 7-3.

There are two different signature combinations for the Corn Exchange Bank, they are: R. P. Pierce as cashier and H. K. Smith as president, and R. P. Pierce as cashier and I. Tucker as president.

There are three different stamps that can be found on the Corn Exchange Bank. The first is a green "Illinois" stamp which can be found vertically placed on the top right. The second is a black stamp that reads "Redeemable at the office of Solon, McElroy & Co. Chicago, Illinois" this can be found on vertically left. Lastly, the third stamp reads "Redeemed in bankable funds by W. H. Rice & Co. Bankers, 63 Clark Street, Chicago, Illinois" vertically on the right in black. All of these stamps are difficult to find and should command a premium.

Often times these stamps are overlooked even by an auction cataloger. With patience one would be able to locate these very interesting stamps.

De Soto – Corn Exchange Bank

Fate: Formerly Western Land & Exchange Co. (Owen 9)
Date: December 12, 1860

Owen Number	Denomination	Plate Position(s)	Basic Info.	Cross Refs.	Rarity
6-1	$1	A-B	Protector: Large 1 in Red Imprint: National Bank Note Co.	Haxby: 20G2a Walton: 1 McKee: 2	R.4

	F	VF	AU	UNC
Issued	$175	-	$350	-
Remainder	-	-	$400	$500
Uncut Remainder Pair	-	$500	-	-

Owen Number	Denomination	Plate Position(s)	Basic Info.	Cross Refs.	Rarity
6-2	$1	A	Protector: Large 1 in Green Imprint: National Note Bank Co.	Haxby: 20G2b Walton: 4 McKee: 1	R.3

	G	VF	AU	UNC
Issued	$80	$160	-	-
Remainder	-	-	$250	$550
"Illinois" Stamp in Green	-	-	-	-
Uncut Remainder Pair	-	-	-	$850

Owen Number	Denomination	Plate Position(s)	Basic Info.	Cross Refs.	Rarity
6-3	$2	A	Protector: in Red	Haxby: 20G4a	R.4
			Imprint: National Note Bank Co.	Walton: 2	
				McKee: 4	

	G	VF	AU	UNC
Issued	-	$300	-	-
Remainder	-	-	$700	$750
Stamp "W. H. Rice & Co."	-	$550	-	-

Owen Number	Denomination	Plate Position(s)	Basic Info.	Cross Refs.	Rarity
6-4	$2	A	Protector: in Green	Haxby: 20G4b	R.3
			Imprint: National Bank Note Co.	Walton: 5	
				McKee: 3	

	G	VF	AU	UNC
Issued	$150	$375	-	-
Remainder	-	$350	$550	$600
"Illinois" Stamp in Green	-	-	-	-
Stamp "Solon, McElroy & Co"	-	-	-	-

Image Courtesy of Heritage Auctions.

Owen Number	Denomination	Plate Position(s)	Basic Info.	Cross Refs.	Rarity
6-5	$3	A	Protector: in Green	Haxby: 20G6b	R.3
			Imprint: National Bank Note Co.	Walton: 6	
				McKee: 5	

	VF	XF	AU	UNC
Issued	-	$400	-	-
Remainder	$100	$350	-	$700
"Illinois" Stamp in Green	-	-	-	-

Owen Number	Denomination	Plate Position(s)	Basic Info.	Cross Refs.	Rarity
6-6	$5	A	Protector: in Red	Haxby: 20G8a	R.7
			Imprint: National Bank Note Co.	Walton: 3	
				McKee: 8	

	F	XF	AU	UNC
Issued	$225	-	-	-
Remainder	-	$560	$700	$900

Owen Number	Denomination	Plate Position(s)	Basic Info.	Cross Refs.	Rarity
6-7	$5	A	Protector: in Green	Haxby: 20G8b	R.3
			Imprint: National Bank Note Co.	Walton: 7	
				McKee: 6	

	VG	F	VF	UNC
Issued	$80	$200	$400	-
Remainder	-	-	-	$800
"Illinois" Stamp in Green	-	-	-	-

Image Courtesy of Heritage Auctions.

Owen Number	Denomination	Plate Position(s)	Basic Info.	Cross Refs.	Rarity
6-8	$1-$1-$2-$5	A-B	Protector: in Red	Haxby: N/A	R.6
			Imprint: Baldwin, Bald & Cousland	Walton: N/A	
				McKee: N/A	

	VF	XF	AU	UNC
Sheet*	-	-	$1100	$1700

*These sheets have only been seen that are signed but not numbered.

Image Courtesy of Heritage Auctions.

Owen Number	Denomination	Plate Position(s)	Basic Info.	Cross Refs.	Rarity
6-9	$1-$1-$2-$3	A-B	Protector: in Green	Haxby: 20X1	R.5
			Imprint: National Bank Note Co	Walton: N/A	
				McKee: N/A	

	VF	XF	AU	UNC
Sheet*	-	$700	$1100	$1700

*All but one of these sheets has been seen numbered but not signed.

De Soto – The Bank of De Soto

Fate: Failed
Date: 1857-63 (notes dated 1863 were note officially released)

Owen Number	Denomination	Plate Position(s)	Basic Info.	Cross Refs.	Rarity
7-1	$1	A-B	Protector: Large ONE in Red Imprint: Baldwin, Bald & Cousland	Haxby: 25G2a Walton: 1 McKee: 1	R.4

	VF	XF	AU	UNC
Issued: 1857-59	$65	$75	$125	-
"Redeemable at 90 Wall St. NY" in Red	-	-	-	-
Stamped "... 90 Wall Street NY" in Red	-	-	$85	$125
Stamped "Bought at 90 Wall St." in Black	$80	-	-	-
Stamped "... at 1 per cent discount" in Blue	$80	-	-	-
Proof	-	-	-	$300

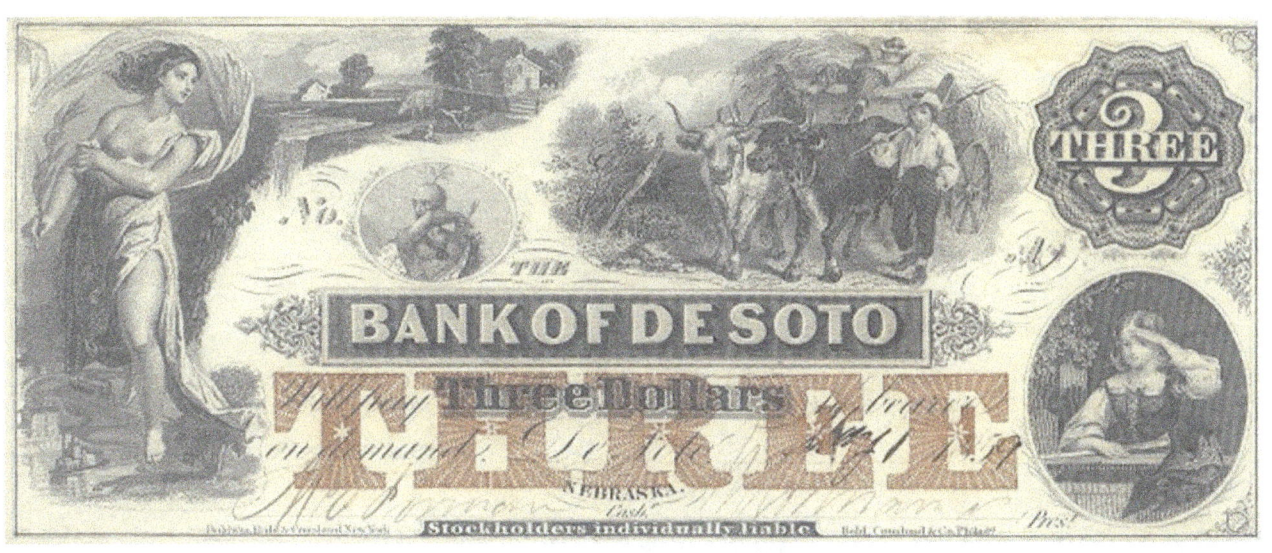

Owen Number	Denomination	Plate Position(s)	Basic Info.	Cross Refs.	Rarity
7-2	$3	A	Protector: Large THREE in Red Imprint: Baldwin, Bald & Cousland	Haxby: 25G6a Walton: 2 McKee: 10	R.4
		VF	XF	AU	UNC
Issued: 1857-59		$90	$110	-	-
1859. "... at No 90 Wall St, NY" in Red		-	-	-	-
1859. Stamped, "Bought at 90 Wall St NY" in Black		-	-	-	-
Proof		-	-	-	$300

Jim McKee Collection

Owen Number	Denomination	Plate Position(s)	Basic Info.	Cross Refs.	Rarity
7-3	$5	A	Protector: Large FIVE in Red Imprint: Baldwin, Bald & Cousland	Haxby: 25G8a Walton: 3 McKee: 13	R.4

	VF	XF	AU	UNC
Issued: 1857-59	$90	$110	-	-
1859. Stamped, "... 90 Wall St NY" in Blue	-	-	-	-
1859. "... at No 90 Wall St NY" in Red	-	-	-	-
1859. "Bought at 90 Wall St NY" in Black	-	-	-	-
Proof	-	-	-	-

51

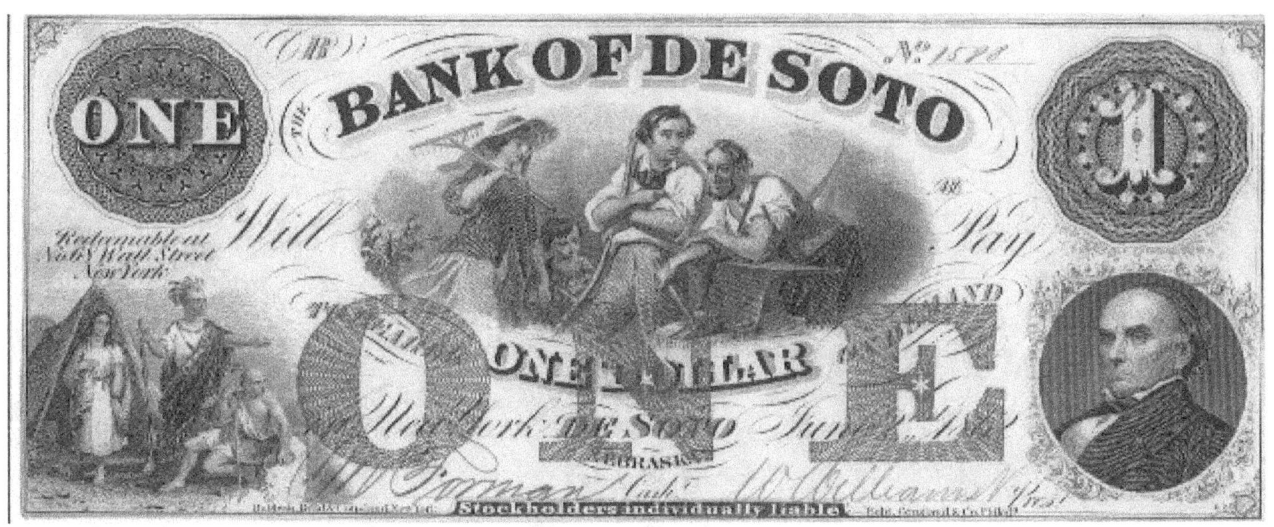

Owen Number	Denomination	Plate Position(s)	Basic Info.	Cross Refs.	Rarity
7-4	$1	A-B	Protector: Large ONE in Green	Haxby: 25G10c	R.4
			Imprint: Baldwin, Bald & Cousland	Walton: 4	
				McKee: 6	

All printed: "Redeemable at No. 68 Wall Street New York" in black at left under ONE.

	F	VF	XF	AU
Issued: 1862	-	$200	-	-
Remainder	-	$85	-	-

Owen Number	Denomination	Plate Position(s)	Basic Info.	Cross Refs.	Rarity
7-5	$2	A	Protector: Large TWO in Green	Haxby: 25G12a	R.5
			Imprint: Baldwin, Bald & Cousland	Walton: 5	
				McKee: 8	

All printed: "Redeemable at No. 68 Wall Street New York" in black at top.

	F	VF	XF	AU
Issued: 1862	-	$125	-	-
Remainder	-	$100	-	-

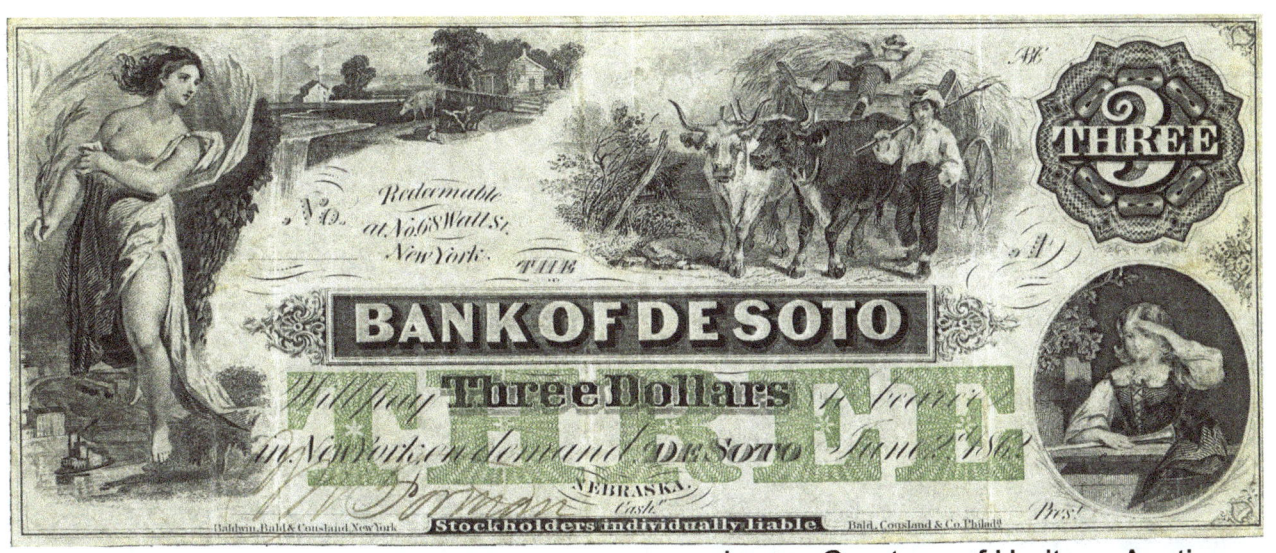

Image Courtesy of Heritage Auctions.

Owen Number	Denomination	Plate Position(s)	Basic Info.	Cross Refs.	Rarity
7-6	$3	A	Protector: Large THREE in Green	Haxby: 25G14c	R.5
			Imprint: Baldwin, Bald & Cousland	Walton: 6	
				McKee: 11	

All printed: Redeemable at No, 68 Wall St. New York" in black at left center between vignettes.

	F	VF	XF	AU
Issued: 1862	-	-	-	-
Remainder	-	$250	-	-

54

Image Courtesy of Heritage Auctions.

Owen Number	Denomination	Plate Position(s)	Basic Info.	Cross Refs.	Rarity
7-7	$1	A-B	Protector: Large ONE in Green Imprint: ABNC	Haxby: 25G2c Walton: 7 McKee: 3	R.1

	VF	XF	AU	UNC
Issued: 1863	-	$50	$70	$125

Image Courtesy of Heritage Auctions.

Owen Number	Denomination	Plate Position(s)	Basic Info.	Cross Refs.	Rarity
7-8	$2	A	Protector: Large TWO in Green Imprint: ABNC	Haxby: 25G4a Walton: 8 McKee: 9	R.1

	VF	XF	AU	UNC
Issued: 1863	-	-	$70	$175

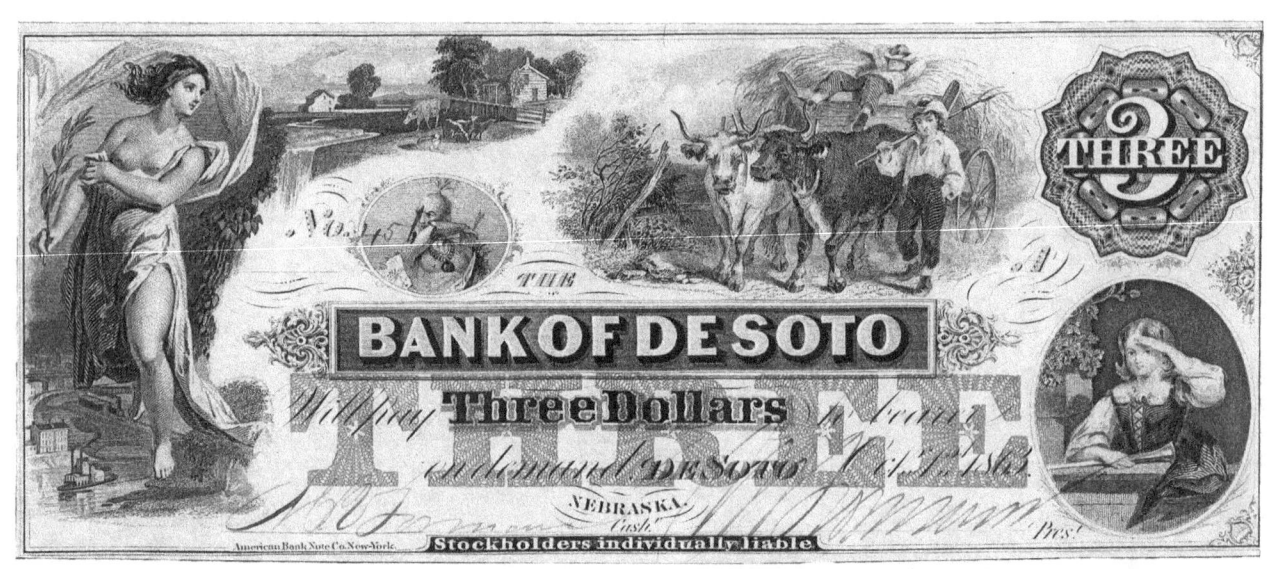

Image Courtesy of Heritage Auctions.

Owen Number	Denomination	Plate Position(s)	Basic Info.	Cross Refs.	Rarity
7-9	$3	A	Protector: Large THREE in Green Imprint: ABNC	Haxby: 25G6c Walton: 9 McKee: 12	R.1

	VF	XF	AU	UNC
Issued: 1863	-	-	$100	$175

Image Courtesy of Heritage Auctions.

Owen Number	Denomination	Plate Position(s)	Basic Info.	Cross Refs.	Rarity
7-10	$1-$1-3$-5	A-B	Protector: None	Haxby: N/A	R.6
			Imprint: Baldwin, Bald & Cousland	Walton: N/A	
				McKee: N/A	

	VF	XF	AU	UNC
Proof Sheet*	-	-	-	$1200

*Six sheets were sold during the Christie's Sale of 1990 some may have been cut down into singles.

De Soto – Desoto Bridge and Ferry Company

Fate: Unknown
Date: 1858-59

NSHS Collection

Owen Number	Denomination	Plate Position(s)	Basic Info.	Cross Refs.	Rarity
8-1	$10	A	Protector: Large TEN in Red Imprint: N/A	Haxby: N/A Walton: N/A McKee: N/A	R.7

	F	VF	AU	UNC
Remainer	-	-	-	-

Little is known about this issuer. It is unclear if these notes helped the ferry business in De Soto or if they were to help bridge the creeks between De Soto and Omaha City.

Waubeek Bank

The Waubeek Bank of De Soto was one of the banks in Nebraska that operated without the benefit of a territorial charter. It opened its doors in 1857 with H.H. Hine as president and A. Castetter as teller. The Waubeek Bank was reported to have issued over $200,000 before "going bust" but this is hard to believe when we take into consideration the scarcity of these notes. One possibility why these notes are more readily available is that there are more altered notes than previously thought.

The employees at the Waubeek Bank were notorious for cutting into the notes when cutting the sheets. This would make a note with full boarders highly desirable. This bank has the most alerted banknotes of all the Nebraska banks during the obsolete time period. Many of the banks hail from the North East.

All notes are signed by C.E Turner (Cashier) and H.H. Hine (President).

Below is a list of the banks that were the final result of Waubeek notes being altered:

    Hartford, CT- Mercantile Bank $5 May 4, 1859
    Decatur, IL- Rail Road Bank $3 Nov. 27, 1857
    Augusta, ME- State Bank $2 Aug. 1, 1857
    Bangor, ME- Mercantile Bank $5 May 1, 1863
    Boston, MA- Bank of North America $3 1857
    Boston, MA- Traders Bank $1 May 1, 1857
    Boston, MA- Bank of Commerce $5 Jan. 24, 1859
    Boston, MA- Bank of Mutual Redemption $5 May 2, 1858
    Boston, MA- Market Bank $5 May 1, 1857
    Boston, MA- Granite Bank $5 May 1, 1857
    Boston, MA- State Bank $5 Jan. 6, 1857
    Danvers, MA- Danvers Bank $3 May 1, 1857
    Holliston, MA- Holliston Bank $5 Jan. 1, 1867
    Hopkinton, MA- Hopkinton Bank $2 May 1, 1857
    Lowell, MA- Rail Road Bank $3 May 1, 1857
    Roxbury, MA- Rockland Bank $2 Oct. 1, 1857
    Roxbury, MA- Rockland Bank $5 May ?, 1857
    Roxbury, MA- Peoples Bank $5 Oct. 1, 1857
    Belvidere, NJ- Belvidere Bank $3 May 14, 1859
    Burlington, NJ- Burlington Bank $5 May 1, 1857
    Camden, NJ- State Bank $5 May 1, 1857
    New York, NY- Peoples Bank $3 Apr. 4, 1859
    Erie, PA- Bank of Commerce $5 Mar. 14, 185
    Pittsburgh, PA-Alleghany Bank $5 July 8, 1959
    Pascoag, RI- Granite Bank $5 Aug. 14, 1857
    Newport, RI- Traders Bank $1 May 1, 1857
    North Providence, RI- Peoples Bank $3 Nov. 1, 1857
    Providence, RI- Bank of Commerce $5 July 10, 1859
    Providence, RI- State Bank $2 Dec. 1, 1857
    Providence, RI- Traders Bank $2 Nov. 2, 1857
    Woonsocket (nee Cumberland), RI- Rail Road Bank $3 July ?, 1857
    Derby Line, VT- Peoples Bank $3 May 4, 1857
    Montpelier, VT- Vermont Bank $3 Oct. 20, 1857

De Soto – Waubeek Bank

Fate: An unauthorized bank - often times used as the base of altered notes
Date: 1857

Owen Number	Denomination	Plate Position(s)	Basic Info.	Cross Refs.	Rarity
9-1	$1	A	Protector: Large ONE in Red Imprint: RWH&E, NEBC	Haxby: 30G2a Walton: 1 McKee: 1	R.4

	VG	VF	AU	UNC
Issued	$50	-	$85	$125
Proprietary Proof	-	-	-	$250

Jim McKee Collection

Owen Number	Denomination	Plate Position(s)	Basic Info.	Cross Refs.	Rarity
9-2	$2	A	Protector: Large TWO in Red Imprint: RWH&E, NEBC	Haxby: 85G4a Walton: 2 McKee: 2	R.3

	VG	VF	AU	UNC
Issued	$50	$75	$130	$225
Proprietary Proof	-	-	-	$250

63

Jim McKee Collection

Owen Number	Denomination	Plate Position(s)	Basic Info.	Cross Refs.	Rarity
9-3	$3	A	Protector: Large THREE in Red Imprint: RWH&E, NEBC	Haxby: 85G6a Walton: 3 McKee: 3	R.3

	VG	VF	AU	UNC
Issued	$40	$100	-	$275
Proprietary Proof	-	-	-	$250

Owen Number	Denomination	Plate Position(s)	Basic Info.	Cross Refs.	Rarity
9-4	$5	A	Protector: Large FIVE in Red Imprint: RWH&E, NEBC	Haxby: 85G8a Walton: 4 McKee: 4	R.3

	VG	VF	AU	UNC
Issued	$65	$100	$300	-
Proprietary Proof	-	-	-	$250

Western Land and Exchange Co.

The Western Land and Exchange Co. was owned by H. Knox Smith and was another bank that operated without a territorial charter. This bank went into business in 1857 and later became the Corn Exchange Bank.

The Corn Exchange Bank also operated without a territorial charter. "The History of Dodge and Washington Counties" states that the Corn Exchange Bank opened in the spring of 1858 by a Chicago firm with I. Tucker as the teller. Signed notes of this bank are signed by R.P. Pierce as the cashier. Some notes carry the signature of H. Knox Smith as the president, while others carry the signature of I. Tucker. The Nebraska Enquirer, of De Soto, Nebraska, made the following announcement about the Corn Exchange Bank on February 14, 1861:

"The Corn Exchange Bank of De Soto is a reality... it was formerly the Western Land and Exchange Company, the change of name was made last summer of which there was due notice given... the Western Land and Exchange Company was chartered in 1857, with the power to change its name at will... H. Knox Smith, the president of said bank, is one of our veritable citizens, and is at all times prepared to redeem all and every one of its issues in specie on presentation."

Leonard M. Owen (the original author of these papers) checked this information in several territorial histories and articles written during this period of time and could find nothing to substantiate the above claim. No record has been found that the Western Land and Exchange Company received a charter from the Territorial Legislature. No record has been found that they ever requested a charter. Many banks received charters that stated that the stock of the bank was assignable and transferable according to such regulation as the directors might think proper.

In effect, this meant that even if the original incorporators were honest and wealthy citizens, the new owners might not be. Also, no charter papers have been located that permit a bank to "change its name at will". This would raise the question of whether the Nebraska Enquirer made a false statement, just failed to research their information, or printed a statement given to them by H. Knox Smith verbatim and without comment. Such are the findings when you research information from the early histories, newspapers, and periodicals.

De Soto – The Western Land and Exchange Co.

Fate: Became The Corn Exchange Bank in De Soto (Owen 6)
Date: 1857

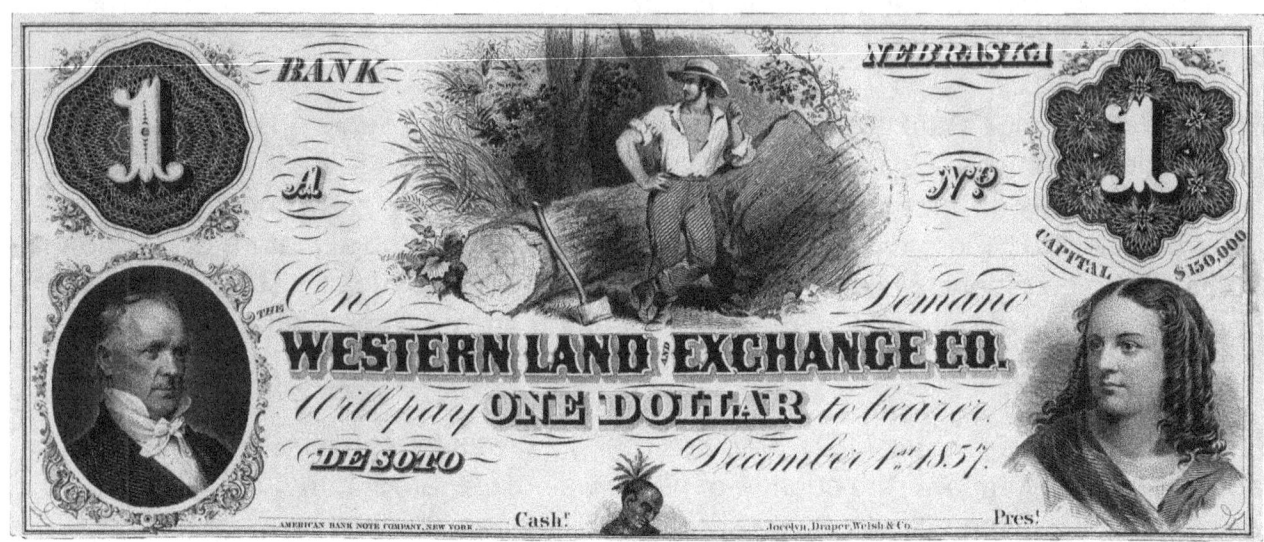

Image Courtesy of Heritage Auctions.

Owen Number	Denomination	Plate Position(s)	Basic Info.	Cross Refs.	Rarity
10-1	$1	A	Protector: None	Haxby: 35G2	R.7
			Imprint: American Bank Note Co. & Jocelyn, Draper, Welsh & Co.	Walton: 1 McKee: 1	

	VF	XF	AU	UNC
Proof	-	$400	-	$700

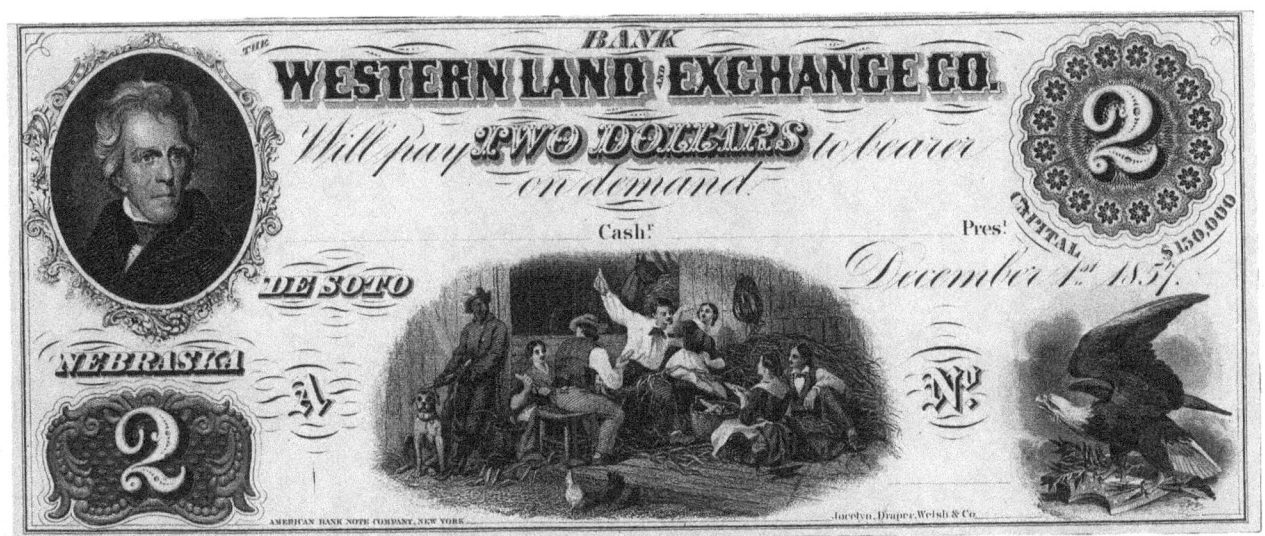

Image Courtesy of Heritage Auctions.

Owen Number	Denomination	Plate Position(s)	Basic Info.	Cross Refs.	Rarity
10-2	$2	A	Protector: None	Haxby: 35G4	R.7
			Imprint: American Bank Note Co. & Jocelyn, Draper, Welsh & Co.	Walton: N/A McKee: N/A	

	VF	XF	AU	UNC
Proof	-	-	-	$1000

NSHS Collection

Owen Number	Denomination	Plate Position(s)	Basic Info.	Cross Refs.	Rarity
10-3	$1-$2	A	Protector: None	Haxby: N/A	R.7
			Imprint: American Bank Note Co. & Jocelyn, Draper, Welsh & Co.	Walton: N/A McKee: N/A	

	VF	XF	AU	UNC
Proof Pair	-	$1500	-	-

Florence

By the mid 1870's Florence was listed as a postal village in Douglas County, Nebraska, on the Missouri River, and on the Omaha & Northwestern Railroad, six miles north of Omaha. Florence has since become a part of the City of Omaha. We will now go back to the start of Florence for a little more information about the part in history played by the village on the eastern border of Nebraska.

Florence had the distinction of being the site of the first white settlement in Douglas County. The Mormons selected this site as their "Winter Quarters" in January 1846. They built a settlement here which they used as their outfitting and supply stopover on their trek west. This site had practically been vacated by the Mormons when the Florence Land Company was organized in the spring of 1854. The organizers were: J.C. Mitchell, J.M. Parker, Phillip Chapmanm B.R. Stuesman, and a few others. The town was surveyed by L.F. Wagner. It was laid out in an area of 270 blocks. History states that at the time Wagner's survey, J.M. Parker started a bank and Florence began to assume metropolitan airs. The Bank of Florence received its charter on January 18, 1856.

The Florence Town Company was organized in 1856, by the organizers of the Land Company and others. Among the "others" was the banking house of Cook, Sargent and Parker of Devenport, Iowa. Soon after the organization of the Town Company, Florence was chartered as a city. Florence became an active candidate for the territorial capitol. Efforts were made to secure the terminal of the Chicago, Rock Island, and Pacific Railroad, which had been surveyed in 1852.

These efforts failed and the railroad company selected Council Bluffs, Iowa as its terminus. Florence failed to secure the railroad terminus or the territorial capitol, and with the failure of the Bank of Florence in the spring of 1858, the growth of Florence declined. Florence remained the starting point for the Mormons to Salt Lake City for several years, and they were responsible for most of the business activity.

The Bank of Florence receieved its charter on January 18, 1856. It was for the usual 25 years with stock of $50,000 to $500,000. The incorporations were listed as H.D. Downey, Levi Harsh, Allan Tomlin, Nathaniel Kilbourn, James C. Mitchell, G.W. Doge and Ebenezer Cook. All of these men had interests in Iowa, and the majority of the notes on the Bank of Florence were circulated in Iowa. Cook, Sargent and Downey had banks in Iowa City, Davenport and Fort Des Moines. The Florence notes could be redeemed at any of these banks.

The Bank of Florence closed its doors in less than two years leaving behind a supply of $100,000 worth of unsigned notes. They arrived after the bank had closed and were never issued nor signed. These notes are still available today in sheets as well as singles and are among the more common of the Nebraska notes. The Book "Banking in Iowa", in referring to the Bank of Florence, says that $200,000 of the notes of this bank was burned in Davenport, Iowa, on September 6, 1858. However, according to "Banker's Almanac 1861" this bank had its original $50,000 in capital and still had an undisclosed amount of notes in circulation. Including Bank of De Soto (Owen 7), Platte Valley Bank (Owen 13), Bank of Nebraska (Owen 15), Bank of Tekama (Owen 22), and Western Marine Insurance Co (Owen 24) there were a total of $600,000 in circulation and the banks retained $100,000 in specie in 1861.

The Bank of Florence notes were printed in sheets of four notes, with the denominations of $1, $2, $3, and $5. The Byron Reed Collection, owned by the City of Omaha, has a $10 note of this bank, but the sheet layout that included this note is not known at this time.

Florence showed steady population growth with 395 residents in 1870 to 1526 citizens in 1910. By 1917 Florence was annexed by the city of Omaha and sits at the north end.

The Bank of Florence was designated a historical landmark on October 14, 1980.

All issued notes where signed by J.M. Parker (Cashier) and George B. Sargent (Pres.). Notes that are fully issued are R.7 while Remaindes are R.1.

Florence – The Bank of Florence

Fate: Failed
Date: 1856-58

Byron Reed Collection

Owen Number	Denomination	Plate Position(s)	Basic Info.	Cross Refs.	Rarity
11-1	$1	A-B	Protector: Large ONE in Red Imprint: Toppan, Carpenter & Co.	Haxby: 40G2a Walton: 1 McKee: 1	R.1

	VG	F	AU	UNC
Issued	-	-	-	-
Remainder	-	-	-	$125

Byron Reed Collection

Owen Number	Denomination	Plate Position(s)	Basic Info.	Cross Refs.	Rarity
11-2	$2	A	Protector: Large TWO in Red Imprint: Toppan, Carpenter & Co.	Haxby: 40G4a Walton: 2 McKee: 2	R.1

	VG	F	AU	UNC
Issued	$100	-	-	-
Remainder	-	-	-	$200
Proprietary Proof*	-	-	-	$100

*Features: Orange Vignettes, and Black counters and Overprint.

Byron Reed Collection

Owen Number	Denomination	Plate Position(s)	Basic Info.	Cross Refs.	Rarity
11-3	$3	A	Protector: Large THREE in Red Imprint: Toppan, Carpenter & Co.	Haxby: 40G6a Walton: 3 McKee: 3	R.1

	VG	F	AU	UNC
Issued	$125	-	-	-
Remainder	-	-	-	$200

Byron Reed Collection

Owen Number	Denomination	Plate Position(s)	Basic Info.	Cross Refs.	Rarity
11-4	$5	A	Protector: Large FIVE in Red Imprint: Toppan, Carpenter & Co.	Haxby: 40G8a Walton: 4 McKee: 4	R.1

	VG	F	AU	UNC
Issued	$300	-	-	-
Remainder	-	-	-	$125

Byron Reed Collection

Owen Number	Denomination	Plate Position(s)	Basic Info.	Cross Refs.	Rarity
11-5	$10	A	Protector: Large TEN in Red Imprint: Toppan, Carpenter & Co.	Haxby: 40G10a Walton: 5 McKee: 5	R.7*

	VF	XF	AU	UNC
Issued	-	-	-	-
Remainder	-	-	-	-

*There is a strong possiblity that this note is unique.

Owen Number	Denomination	Plate Position(s)	Basic Info.	Cross Refs.	Rarity
11-6	$1-$2-$3-$5*	A	Protector: Large VALUE in Red	Haxby: 40X1	R.3
				Walton: N/A	
			Imprint: Toppan, Carpenter & Co.	McKee: N/A	

	VF	XF	AU	UNC
Remainder Sheet	-	$160	$335	$400

*Proof Pairs have started to show up at auction either $1-$2 or $3-$5 in AU: $175.

Lincoln

None were ever officially issued. After researching the Lincoln City Council minutes and found that they decided to abandon the project even before the notes were delivered. They did pay the printing bill and when the notes arrived they were placed in the vault of State National Bank (whose President was a member of the Council). During a 1890s remodeling of the bank the notes were "found" and ended up on the streets as souvenirs. A few were spuriously signed and crumpled to look aged and spent. This drew the attention of the Secret Service who sent an agent to the City to gather up what notes he could. Obviously he didn't get that many given the survival. I have seen signed examples but none with what would have been the correct names and date.

There were four people authorized to speak with bank note companies: E. E. Brown (Mayor - and would be seen on each note), J. J. Gosper (McGosper), S. G. Owen, and L. A. Scoggin. The last three anyone of them could have signed as clerk. There is also a chance that the clerk could be from another person. Either way this researcher and those before him haven't see a Lincoln note with appropriate signatures. The key signature is the mayor's.

Lincoln – The City of Lincoln

Fate: Never issued, Secret Service later obtained then destroyed
Date: 1870s

Image Courtesy of Heritage Auctions.

Owen Number	Denomination	Plate Position(s)	Basic Info.	Cross Refs.	Rarity
12-1	$1	N/A	Protector: None	Haxby: N/A	R.6
			Imprint: Baldwin, Bald & Cousland	Walton: N/A	
				McKee: 1	

	G	VG	F	VF
Spurious	$75	$110	-	-
Remainder	-	-	$150	$300
Proof	-	-	-	-

Owen Number	Denomination	Plate Position(s)	Basic Info.	Cross Refs.	Rarity
12-2	$2	N/A	Protector: None	Haxby: N/A	R.6
			Imprint: Baldwin, Bald & Cousland	Walton: N/A	
				McKee: 2	

	VG	VF	XF	AU
Spurious	$100	$500	-	-
Remainder	$150	$350	-	-
Proof	-	-	-	-

Image Courtesy of Heritage Auctions.

Owen Number	Denomination	Plate Position(s)	Basic Info.	Cross Refs.	Rarity
12-3	$1-$2	N/A	Protector: None	Haxby: N/A	R.7
			Imprint: Baldwin, Bald & Cousland	Walton: N/A	
				McKee: N/A	

	VF	XF	AU	UNC
Proof Sheet	-	-	-	$1150

Nebraska City

On March 2, 1855, the Territorial Legislature approved the incorporation of Nebraska City and it was declared to be the seat of justice for Otoe County. An election was held in May of 1855 to select the town officers and Dr. Henry Bradford became the first Mayor of Nebraska City. The municipal years were decided to begin on June 1 of each year and Mayor Bradford was re-elected for another term of office in 1856. Mayor Bradford registered Nebraska City as a town at the land office in Omaha on March 31, 1857.

Nebraska City consolidated with the towns of Kearney, South Nebraska City, and Parairie City in 1858, with A.A. Brookfield as mayor of the new Nebraska City.

The Kearney mentioned about was the site of the Old Fort Kearney which was established in 1844. This fort was used by the government until it was abandoned in 1848 by the movement of the garrison to New Fort, Kearney, on the Platte River, in the south central part of the state. The abandoned fort was left in charge of a Mr. Hardin.

He was followed a year later by Col. John Boulware who had established himself at Fort Calhoun in 1826 and had moved to Old Fort Kearney in 1846, where he established a government ferry. His business ventures were exceedingly profitable and it was the short term loan of $10,000 in gold that made it possible for the Platte Valley Bank to survive the panic of 1857.

When the U.S. Government withdrew all claim to Old Fort Kearney, John Boulware, John B. Boulware, and Hiram P. Downs secured special permits from the Secretary of the Interior to remain at the site of Nebraska City, as this was considered Indian Lands, until the spring of 1854. The above men claimed the site of Fort Kearney and Nebraska City as settlers, claimants, and squatters.

The Boulware's claimed the site of Old Fort Kearney and Mr. Downs claimed that portion that was to become the original Nebraska City. In April of 1854, Stephen F. Nuckolls arrived on the scene, followed by Allen A. Bradford in May of the same year. They made an arrangement with Mr. Downs to be partners on his claim, which became the Nebraska City Town Company. This company later added the following names to its list of members: H.P. Bennett, William B Hail, Lafayette Nuckolls, John Doniphan, L.D. Bird, James Doniphan, S.E. Frazer, Marshall and Woodward, N.B. Giddings, Charles F. Holly, J.W. Kelly, W.S. VanDoren, Robert Cook, and J. Sterling Morton.

In the A.T. Andreas "History of 1882," we find the following: "All or most of these men secured a goodly number of corner lots, there being as many of these as it was within the scope of mathematical possibilities to create."

The fist hotel was built by Mr. Downs in the fall of 1854 and it was known as the City Hotel. The second hotel was built by Col. John McMecham and was known as the Planters' House. Table Creek Post Office was established in 1852 with Col. Boulware as the postmaster. He was followed in 1853 by Hiram P. Downs as postmaster, and the name was changed to the Nebraska City Post Office the following year, with C.W. Pierce as the postmaster. The first preacher was a Methodist missionary by the name of William D. Gage, who arrived in 1853. The first child to be born was the son of George H. Benton, who was born in August of 1854.

The first slaves were brought to Nebraska City by Stephen F. Nuckolls in the fall of 1854. The slaves were two females and two males by the name of Shade and Shack. Shade and the two females escaped to Chicago with the help of the underground railway. After the Civil War, Shade became a member of the South Carolina Legislature.

Judge Charles F. Holly brought a male and a female slave to Nebraska but was forced to sell them to a man from Missouri to pay a debt owed to William B. Hail.

Alexander Majors brought five house servants with him from Missouri in 1857. Three of these, all girls, escaped to Chicago with the help of the underground railway in June 1860. Robert Kirkum had one female slave which with the above mentioned slaved constituted the slave population of Nebraska City.

John Brown established a way station of the underground railway in Nebraska City and this may account for the high percentage of runaway slaves in this area. John Brown's Cave is still an attraction today in Nebraska City.

William and Kennett McLennan operated a steam ferry boat at Nebraska City from about July of 1854 until it was sunk in Plattsmouth in 1858 or 1859. Stephen F. Nuckolls erected a saw mill in 1854 which operated for a short period of time.

Judge Hardin, in November of 1855, presided over the first criminal case in Nebraska City, which was the Territory against James W. Woods for selling intoxicating liquors. The first brick building in Nebraska City was built on the corner of Fifth and Main Streets in the fall of 1854. It was built by Stephen F. Nuckolls to be used as the State House. It was hoped that Nebraska City might become the capitol of the Territory. Mr. Nuckolls used this house as his residence until 1856 when it became the home of the Platte Valley Bank.

A quote from Andreas' "History of the State of Nebraska" about the panic of 1857 follows: "When John Thomson failed in New York, and the Ohio Life and Trust Company in Cincinnati; when all banks all over the country began to go down, the merchants of St. Louis – with which city nearly all Nebraska transactions were conducted – placed the various promises to pay in the hands of one of their number to collect. Going first to Florence, he took what the Bank of Florence had, and its doors closed.

So with Omaha and Bellevue, both unable to stand the demand made upon them. Hourly expected at Nebraska City by steamer, the officers and friends of the bank endeavored to arrange a plan of action to secure at least a temporary delay. The whistle of the steamer was heard, the doors closed, the president and cashier literally "took to the bush." With saddlebags on his arm, the St. Louis man came up the street, reaching the bank to find Mr. George W. Sroat on the steps composedly awaiting his approach. Where was the cashier? – didn't know. The president? – didn't know. Would the bank open soon? Mr. Sroat supposed that it would. The steamer whistled again and the stranger, after inquiring if he could get back by stage in the morning, broke for the boat and passed on to Brownville. The time gained was used to the best advantage. John Bellevue, though anything but a friend of S.F. Nuckolls, the president, opened his safe doors and gave up his gold to extent of $10,000. Others contributed, and at the regular time of opening the counter of the Platte Valley Bank was a sight to make a miser glad. The stage came in, and with it the stranger, saddlebags and all.

He remarked that he had some bills that he wished to redeem. Joshua Garside, the cashier, replied that they were trying to get in their issue, and he was glad of the opportunity to take up so large an amount at ounce. The stranger looked at the gold, at his saddlebags, and remarked that the former was very heavy; that he had a long journey before him, and finally, that if the bank had the money, he guessed he didn't' want it!

The borrowed money was returned, and that afternoon $2,000 in bills presented for payment, would have placed this bank with its contemporaries – amount those things which were, but are not."

The Nebraska City News was the first newspaper for Nebraska City. It was owned by S.F. Nuckolls, H.F. Downs, and A.A. Bradford. These gentlemen were also the owners of the town site. The first edition was actually printed in Sidney, Iowa, on November 14, 1854. Dr. Henry Bradford was the first editor. All other issues were printed in Nebraska City. Thomas Morton bought the paper in 1855 and J. Sterling Morton became the editor at the wage of $50.00 per month.

The Nebraska Press – The People's Press was established in the spring of 1858. This paper changed hands many times in the first several years and the name was changed each time.

Some of the other names of the paper were as follows: Press and Herald, The Press, Daily Press, Press Printing Company, Nebraska Press, Press and Chronicle, and The Press. A German paper was started in Nebraska City in 1861 by the name of the Nebraska Deutzch Zeitung. This name was changed to Staats Zeitung in 1867.

Arbor lodge State Historical Park in Nebraska City was the home of J. Sterling Morton. It is at the west edge of town. It is a 52-room mansion on an area of 65 acres. The whole area is a park with rose garden, arboretum, carriage house, and more than 200 varieties of trees and shrubs. Morton originated the idea of setting aside a special day for tree planting. Arbor Day began in Nebraska in 1872 and has been observed in Nebraska on Morton's birthday, April 22, since 1885.

The Platte Valley Bank of Nebraska City received its charter from the Territorial Legislature on January 18, 1856. The charter was for the usual 25 years, with the following as the owners: J.W. Coolidge, J.C. Campbell, H. Joy, S.F. Nuckolls, J. Boulware Sr., A.A. Bradford, W.B. Hail, William Larimer Jr., and I.L. Gibbs.

This is the only "Chartered" bank that redeemed all of the notes presented at par, which would indicate that the officers of this bank were operating a legitimate banking enterprise.

After the panic had became wide-spread, the Nebraska City News reported that $40,000 in redeemed notes of this bank had been burned, with $65,000 having been burned previously for a total of redeemed and destroyed notes of $105,000. This accounts for the extreme rarity of the notes of this bank. However, according to "Banker's Almanac 1861" this bank had its original $50,000 in capital and still had an undisclosed amount of notes in circulation. Including Bank of De Soto (Owen 7), Bank of Florence (Owen 11), Bank of Nebraska (Owen 15), Bank of Tekama (Owen 22), and Western Marine Insurance Co (Owen 24) there were a total of $600,000 in circulation and the banks retained $100,000 in specie in 1861. By 1863 this bank only had $16,000 in circulation.

On every issued note you can find the signature of President S.F. Nuckolls while the Cashier is unidentified at this time. The "Banker's Almanac" lists J. Garside as the cashier on file.

The Platte Valley Bank was well thought of by the St. Louis banking institutions, as well as the local banks and newspapers of the day.

Notes of this bank are known in the following denominations: $1, $2, and $10. The $5 denomination is also known, but in proof only.

Nebraska City – McCann & Metcalf* (Private Bankers)**

Fate: Closed
Date: 1861-63

NSHS Collection

Owen Number	Denomination	Plate Position(s)	Basic Info.	Cross Refs.	Rarity
13-1	$1	N/A	Protector: None	Haxby: N/A	R.7
			Imprint: N/A	Walton: N/A	
				McKee: N/A	

	G	VG	F	VF
Issued	-	-	-	-

*Not much is known about this bank other than what we see on the note itself.
**For a more complete list of private bankers see Appendix B

The Platte Valley Bank of Nebraska City, A One Year Success

After a year, when banking in Nebraska was declared an illegal business by the territorial legislature, the need for such institutions became obvious. Being isolated without even basic railroad service, Nebraska was also a magnet for banks partially because clearing their "issued" currency took weeks or even months particularly when circulation occurred hundreds of miles away. Some said all it took to open a bank was a few "businessmen" who had enough capital to print a bunch of banknotes which they spent anyway they could.

John Boulware settled in Nebraska at Fort Atkinson and in 1846 established a ferry service Table Creek primarily servicing Old Fort Kearny on the site of today's Nebraska City. He was joined by Stephen F. Nuckolls and several other local businessmen who applied to the territorial legislature for a banking charter in 1858. Because Boulware and three of the other incorporators were in the legislature it proved not too difficult to obtain a 25 year charter for their Platte Valley Bank which authorized the issuance of $500,000 in stock on January 18, 1856.

Newspaper articles disagree as to whether the original bank was to be in a house built by Nuckolls at 5th and Main Streets or a purpose-built three-story masonry building which he constructed for the bank, an Odd Fellows Hall and several attorney and insurance offices. Although it had been intended to open the bank in June of 1856 it did not actually start until November 10. The Platte Valley bank opened to glowing press with the Brownville Nebraska Advertiser claiming that one could find as much as "$30,000 in American gold and $20,000 in silver, foreign gold and eastern drafts" in its vaults.

1857 proved to be an impossible year for all Nebraska "issuing" banks. When rumors began circulating that the Platte Valley Bank was in trouble depositors panicked. Mr. Nuckolls told depositors, eager to withdraw their accounts, that a steamboat of coin was about to arrive from St. Louis. When the boat docked a man carried two heavy bags to the bank and announced "there it is if you really want it." Since the depositors saw that their fears were groundless, they left. Interestingly, the bags contained only washers intended for an Omaha hardware store.

At another point a robbery which implicated bank officers started a similar run on the bank. Thomas Morton, owner of the Nebraska News plunked down a deposit of gold and silver and again the bank was saved.

With a major nationwide depression in 1857, a group of St. Louis businessmen gathered up all of the various Nebraska banknotes they had accumulated and sent a collector to get whatever gold and silver the banks had on hand. The agent took a steamboat up to Florence and worked his way down the river through Omaha and Bellevue. As the Platte Valley Bank was warned of his imminent arrival, the bank was closed with George Sroat left on the steps. When the gentleman approached with empty saddlebags, Sroat said the cashier had just left but would return the following morning. The agent left for Brownville on the steamboat promising to return the next day's stagecoach. This enabled Boulware to borrow $10,000 of gold from Nuckolls' safe. When the agent returned the following day and saw the pile of gold he figured the bank was in good shape and decided not to try and transport the heavy gold by horseback, planning to return by boat at a still later date. The gold was returned and the bank saved again.

By March of 1858 the St. Louis clearing house announced that the only Nebraska banknotes they would accept were Platte Valley Bank's. That June the Nebraska City News reported a strange "fire broke out in front of the bank…the work of an incendiary and strong suspicion rests on two or three officers and directors who were seen to throw turpentine on the flames." The officers were in fact publicly burning all of the unissued and redeemed notes on the bank, saving the stockholders and depositors from the ruin experienced by many others throughout the territory.

When all was said and done, the Platte Valley Bank, though it survived only about a year, was the only territorial bank to redeem all of its outstanding notes at par, the only such bank to survive the 1857 depression and the last chartered territorial bank to close its doors. By Nebraska's statehood in 1867 all of the wildcat banks who issued notes were gone with only their banknotes, now greatly sought by collectors, remaining as reminders of a nearly universal failed banking experiment.

Nebraska City – The Platte Valley Bank

Fate: Closed
Date: 1856-60

Jim McKee Collection

Owen Number	Denomination	Plate Position(s)	Basic Info.	Cross Refs.	Rarity
13-1	$1	A-B	Protector: Large ONE in Red Imprint: Toppan, Carpenter & Co.	Haxby: 45G2a Walton: 1 McKee: 1	R.7

	G	VG	F	VF
Issued	$250	$600	-	-
Remainder	-	-	-	-

Image Courtesy of Heritage Auctions.

Owen Number	Denomination	Plate Position(s)	Basic Info.	Cross Refs.	Rarity
13-2	$2	A	Protector: Large 2 in Red Imprint: Toppan, Carpenter & Co.	Haxby: 45G4a Walton: 2 McKee: 2	R.7

		G	VG	F	VF
Issued		$250	-	-	-

Image Courtesy of Heritage Auctions.

Owen Number	Denomination	Plate Position(s)	Basic Info.	Cross Refs.	Rarity
13-3	$5	A	Protector: Large 5 in Red Imprint: Toppan, Carpenter & Co.	Haxby: 45G6a Walton: 3 McKee: 3	R.7

	G	VG	F	VF
Issued	-	$700	-	-
Proof*	-	-	-	-

Haxby does not list an issued or remander note type - only a proof (G6a).

Image Courtesy of Heritage Auctions.

Owen Number	Denomination	Plate Position(s)	Basic Info.	Cross Refs.	Rarity
13-4	$10	A	Protector: Large TEN in Red Imprint: Toppan, Carpenter & Co.	Haxby: 45G8a Walton: 4 McKee: N/A	R.7

	G	VG	F	VF
Issued	-	-	-	-
Remainder	-	-	$800	-

Nemaha City

These rare notes were interest bearing-notes at 20% per-annum, and issued in $1, $2, $3, and $5 with a total issuance of $1,000. There are no records that have been found that can prove that these notes were ever issued. Thus, the only notes in the market are remainders. C.E.L. Holmes owned the second sawmill in Nemaha City. The mill was in operation for about a year (1858-59). It can be assumed that these notes were meant to fund the sawmill to keep it operational. Mr Holmes was appointed County Chair from 1859-77.

The other names on the notes are that of George Brownlee, a business man who hailed from Indiana. Mr. Brownlee who opened the second store in Nemaha City in late 1856, but by the spring of 1857 the store was sold to creditors from Cincinnati. A year and half later Mr. Brownlee came into legal troubles because he (and his business partner Mr. Moore) did not repay a promissory note dated May 2, 1857 for $1067.87. This can be assumed this money was to help keep the store in business as Mr. Brownlee and Mr. Moore promised to pay nine months after with 10% per-annum.

The only known sheets are of the $1 and the $2, theoretically there could be full sheets as well as $3 and $5 uncut pair sheets.

Nemaha City – C.E.L. Holmes

Fate: Never Issued
Date: 1858-59

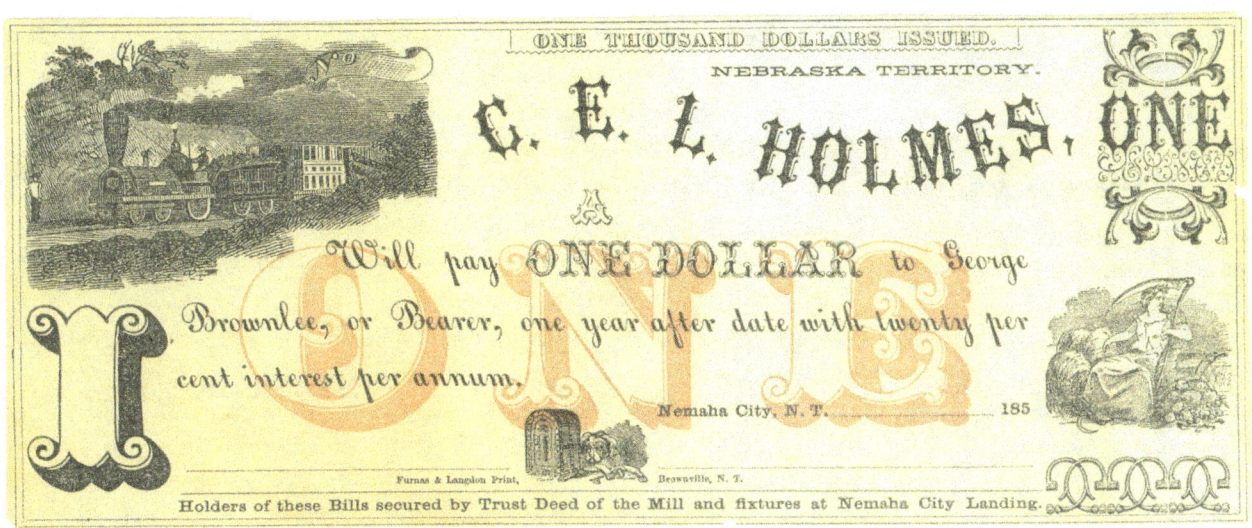

NSHS Collection

Owen Number	Denomination	Plate Position(s)	Basic Info.	Cross Refs.	Rarity
14-1	$1	A	Protector: Large ONE in Red Imprint: Furnas & Langdon	Haxby: N/A Walton: 1 McKee: 1	R.7

	G	VG	F	VF
Remainder	-	-	-	-

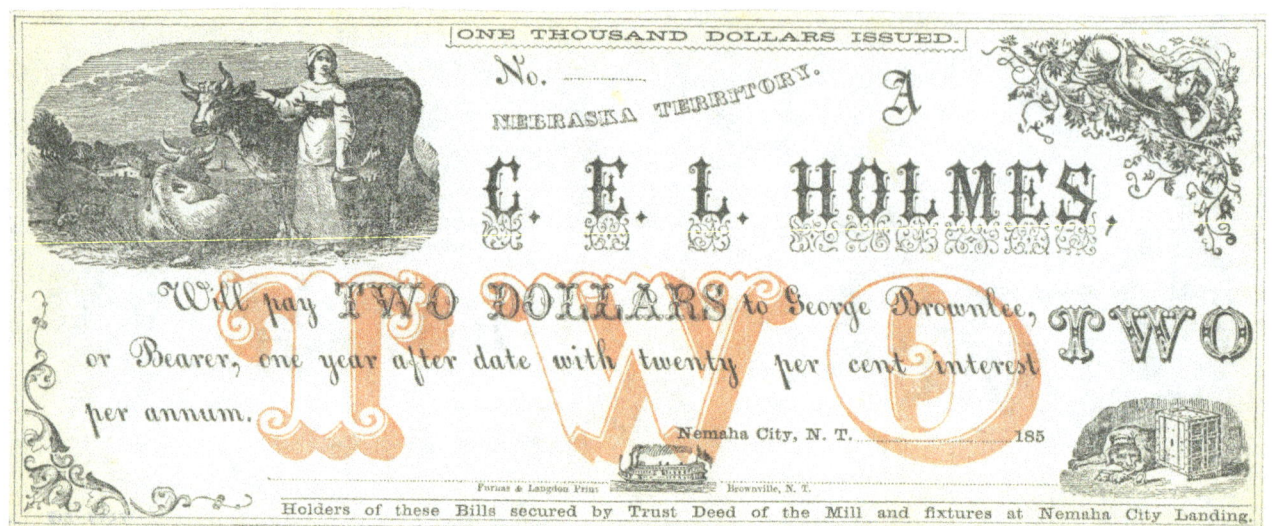

NSHS Collection

Owen Number	Denomination	Plate Position(s)	Basic Info.	Cross Refs.	Rarity
14-2	$2	A	Protector: Large TWO in Red Imprint: Furnas & Langdon	Haxby: N/A Walton: 2 McKee: 2	R.7

	G	VG	F	VF
Remainder	-	-	-	-

NSHS Collection

Owen Number	Denomination	Plate Position(s)	Basic Info.	Cross Refs.	Rarity
14-3	$3	A	Protector: Large THREE in Red Imprint: Furnas & Langdon	Haxby: N/A Walton: 3 McKee: 3	R.7

	G	VG	F	VF
Remainder	-	-	-	-

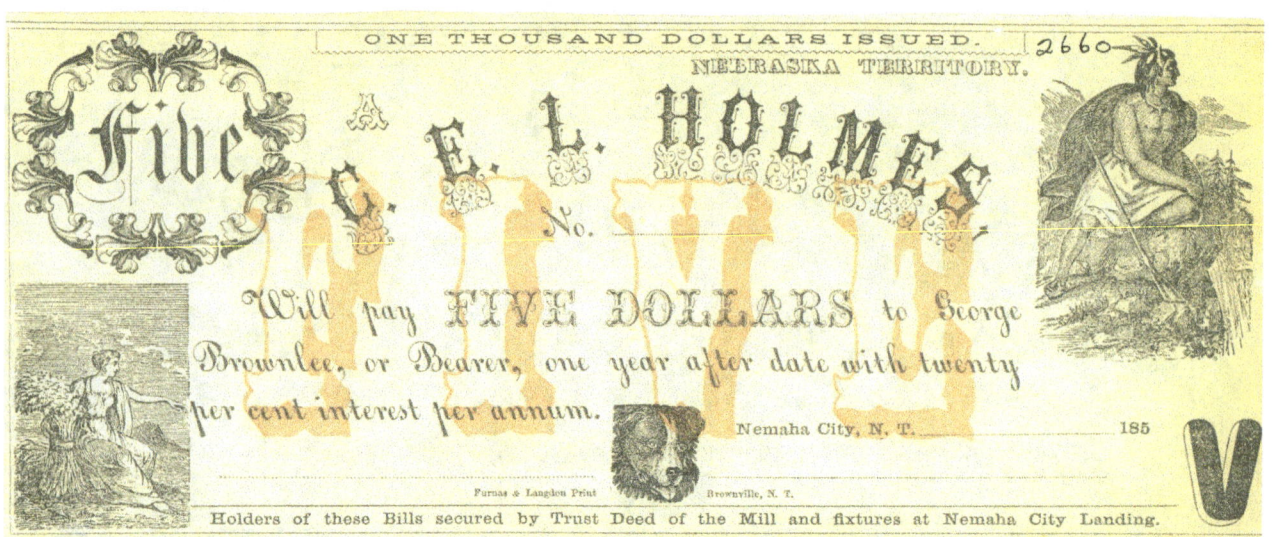

NSHS Collection

Owen Number	Denomination	Plate Position(s)	Basic Info.	Cross Refs.	Rarity
14-4	$5	A	Protector: Large FIVE in Red Imprint: Furnas & Langdon	Haxby: N/A Walton: 4 McKee: 4	R.7

	G	VG	F	VF
Remainder	-	-	-	-

Image Courtesy of Heritage Auctions.

Owen Number	Denomination	Plate Position(s)	Basic Info.	Cross Refs.	Rarity
14-5	$1-$2	A	Protector: Large VALUE in Red Imprint: Furnas & Langdon	Haxby: N/A Walton: N/A McKee: N/A	R.7

	G	VG	AU	UNC
Remainder	-	-	-	$1750

Omaha

Omaha, or "Omaha City" as it was originally known, was surveyed in June and July of 1854. The surveyor was Mr. A.D. Jones, who was assisted my Mr. C.H. Downs. The city was surveyed in an area of 332 blocks, with each block 264 feet square. All streets were 100 feet wide with the exception of Capitol Avenue which was given a width of 120 feet. An area of 600 square feet was laid out on Capitol Hill that was known as Capitol Square.

Many of the residents of Council Bluffs, Iowa, attended a picnic on Capitol Hill in celebration of the 4th of July. Many of these Council Bluff residents became residents of the new town known as "Omaha City".

From the above account, it would appear that "Omaha City" was started in June or July of 1854. However, preliminary groundwork had been set in motion prior to this time. Mr. William D. Brown, a resident and business man from Council Bluffs, and owner of the Lone Tree Ferry, had for some time been impressed by the plateau that was later to become "Omaha City". Mr. Brown had been over the ground many times during his travels between Council Bluffs and the Nebraska side of the Missouri River, while bringing people across the river on their travels to the gold fields of California and other western endeavors.

Mr. Brown suggested that he and some of his friends check into the possibility of setting up a town site on the Nebraska side of the river. Mr. Brown, Dr. Enos Lowe, Jesse Lowe, Jesse Williams, Joseph H.D. Street, and others organized the "Council Bluffs and Nebraska Steam Ferry Company" on July 23, 1853. They intended to secure the town site when Nebraska was admitted as a Territory. Nebraska was admitted as a Territory on May 23, 1854.

Mr. A.D. Jones, Thomas Allen, and William Allen crossed the river in the fall of 1853 to secure claims on the Nebraska side. Each located a claim according to squatter laws of the time. They were notified by Mr. Hepner, the Indian agent that they would have to leave their claims as the land was still owned by the Indians.

The Indians signed the documents to yield title to this land in the month of March and April, 1854, which made the actions described in the first part of this section possible.

The name "Omaha" was selected by the ferry company as the name for "Omaha City". The name was selected from the nearest Indian tribe in the area, which was the tribe known as the Omahas.

The Indian meaning of the word Omahas is "Above all others on a stream".

After the town site had been surveyed, the ferry company looked to task of erecting buildings. A brickyard was started by Benjamin Winchester to make bricks for the building of the Capitol and other buildings. This venture failed and the bricks for the Territorial Capitol had to be hauled from Kanesville (later to be known as Council Bluffs).

Some of the first settlers in "Omaha City" were Benjamin Winchester, Mr. and Mrs. Newell, Mr. and Mrs. William P. Snowden, the Cam Reeves family, P.G. Peterson, Mr. and Mrs. Bedell, and others. Many of the early settlers did not permanently settle in "Omaha City" until the fall of 1855 as they built homes for their families before moving them from Council Bluffs.

The Bank of Nebraska

The following men were listed as the organizers of the Bank of Nebraska: Benjamin F. Allen, Benjamin R. Pegram, Hoyt Sherman, Louden Mullin, George Jennings, Reuben Sypher, and Frank R. West. The officers were: Benjamin F. Allen, president; Samuel Moffat, cashier; and David H. Moffat, assistant cashier. While only B.F. Allen and S. Moffatt's signatures are the only ones to appear on the Bank of Nebraska notes as President and Cashier respectively.

The Bank of Nebraska received its charter on January 18, 1856. This charter was for the usual 25 years, with capital stock set at $50,000 to $500,000 and a subscription of $50,000 necessary to open.

According to "Banker's Almanac 1861" this bank had its original $50,000 in capital and still had an undisclosed amount of notes in circulation. Including Bank of De Soto (Owen 7), Bank of Florence (Owen 11), Bank of Nebraska (Owen 15), Bank of Tekama (Owen 22), and Western Marine Insurance Co (Owen 24) there were a total of $600,000 in circulation and the banks retained $100,000 in specie in 1861.

The notes for this bank were furnished by two different printers. The first type was printed by Toppan, Carpenter & Co., and the signed notes bear the signatures of B.F. Allen and S. Moffat. These notes were printed in sheets of four notes, with the denominations of $1, $1, $2 and $5. These are the only denominations known for general circulation purposes but a $10 proof note is known.

The second type of note was printed by Bald, Cousland & Company. These notes were signed by B.R. Pegram as the president and D.C. DeForest as the cashier, as they became the holders of these offices in 1858. This type of note is found in the denominations of $1 and $2.

Omaha – The Bank of Nebraska

Fate: Failed
Date: 1856-60

Image Courtesy of Heritage Auctions.

Owen Number	Denomination	Plate Position(s)	Basic Info.	Cross Refs.	Rarity
15-1	$1	A-B	Protector: Large 1 in Red Imprint: Toppan, Carpenter & Co	Haxby: 55G2a Walton: 1 McKee: 1	R.6

	VG	F	VF	XF
Issued	-	$300	-	-
B.F. Allen Stamp in Blue	$250	-	-	-

Owen Number	Denomination	Plate Position(s)	Basic Info.	Cross Refs.	Rarity
15-2	$1	A	Protector: Large ONE in Red Imprint: Baldwin, Bald & Cousland	Haxby: 55G4a Walton: 5 McKee: 2	R.5

	VG	F	AU	UNC
Issued	-	$150	-	-
Remainder	-	$150	-	-
Proof	-	-	-	$425

Image Courtesy of Heritage Auctions.

Owen Number	Denomination	Plate Position(s)	Basic Info.	Cross Refs.	Rarity
15-3	$2	A	Protector: Large 2 in Red Imprint: Toppan, Carpenter & Co	Haxby: 55G6a Walton: 2 McKee: 3	R.7

	VG	F	VF	XF
Issued	$550	-	-	-

Owen Number	Denomination	Plate Position(s)	Basic Info.	Cross Refs.	Rarity
15-4	$2	A	Protector: Large TWO in Red Imprint: Baldwin, Bald & Cousland	Haxby: 55G8a Walton: 2 McKee: 4	R.5

	VG	F	VF	UNC
Issued	-	$100	-	-
Remainder	-	$150	-	-
Proof	-	-	-	$500

Owen Number	Denomination	Plate Position(s)	Basic Info.	Cross Refs.	Rarity
15-5	$5	N/A	Protector: Large 5 in Red	Haxby: 55G10a	R.7
			Imprint: Toppan, Carpenter & Co	Walton: 3	
				McKee: 5	

	VF	XF	AU	UNC
Remainder	-	-	-	-

Picture is in grayscale. A color scan is needed.

Owen Number	Denomination	Plate Position(s)	Basic Info.	Cross Refs.	Rarity
15-6	$10	N/A	Protector: None	Haxby: 55G12	R.7
			Imprint: Toppan, Carpenter & Co	Walton: 4	
				McKee: 6	

	VF	XF	AU	UNC
Proof	-	-	-	-

Picture is in grayscale. A color scan is needed.

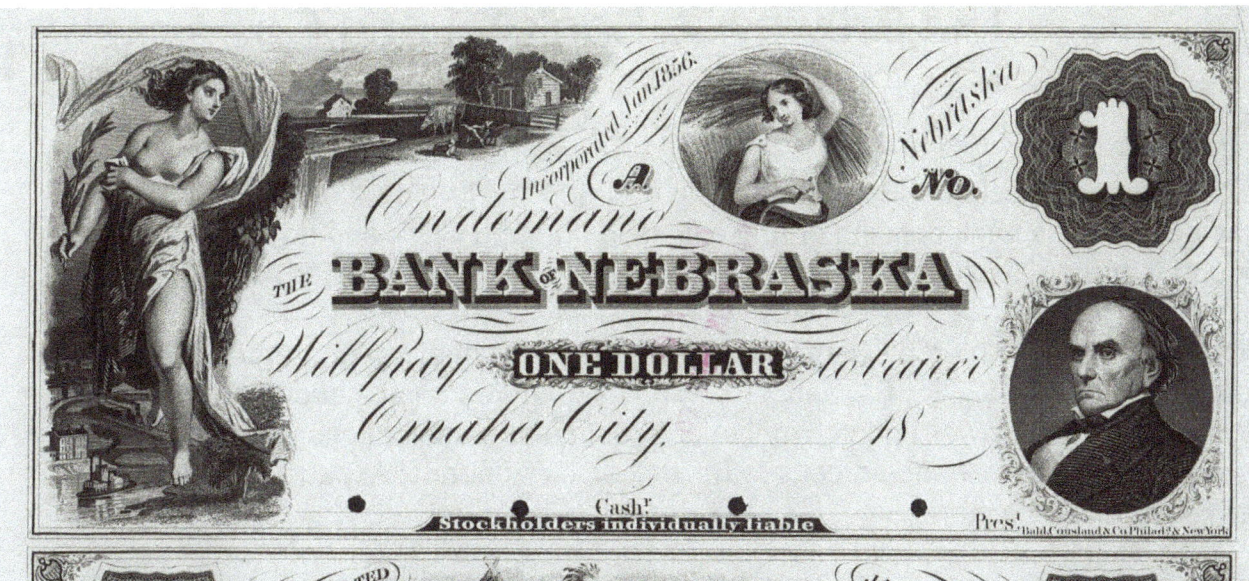

Image Courtesy of Heritage Auctions.

Owen Number	Denomination	Plate Position(s)	Basic Info.	Cross Refs.	Rarity
15-7	$1-$2	A	Protector: None	Haxby: N/A	R.7
			Imprint: Baldwin, Bald & Cousland	Walton: N/A	
				McKee: N/A	

	VF	XF	AU	UNC
Proof Pair	-	-	-	$1300

The Brownville Bank & Land Co.

Little is known about the Brownville Bank & Land Co. No record has been found that they ever had a bank building or any offices in "Omaha City", and no record has been found that they applied for a charter to do business in Nebraska Territory.

The notes were printed by Danforth, Wright & Co., in sheets of four notes, with the denominations of $3, $5, $5, and $10. Many signatures combinations are found on these notes. They were printed in five different color combinations with red-brown, green, brown, yellow and no color lathework. See Appendix A (page 167) for an example of each color.

These different colors may have been used because they were to have been circulated in different localities. These notes were not actually a Nebraska issue but the notes stated that they were payable on demand at Omaha City, Nebraska. These notes also heavily circulated in Bloomington, Illinois and Janesville, Wisconsin.

All notes have stamped serial numbers and are engraved with the date September 1, 1857. Occasionally you will come across a remainder; this type will not be priced in this edition. In both McKee's and Walton's book they list the sheet colors as 'brown' and 'yellow'. I have yet to see a yellow sheet (although that doesn't mean they aren't out there). What has been seen are uncut 'yellow' proof pairs (a $3-$5 both with plate position A) printed on card stock. These go for around $900 in Gem UNC. What I do see are 'green' and 'brown' and one 'red-brown' proof sheet on card from the Christies sale in 1990. This proof sheet is more than likely already cut down as a $3 'red-brown' proof has already came to auction (Baltimore 2011) and realized $6,325. In 1990 the proof sheet sold for $3,850. It's possible that (a) all the yellow sheets where cut down into singles (b) they both meant 'green' (c) they never saw the 'green' sheets and all the 'yellow' sheets are either cut down or stored away or (d) some weird mixture of all the above.

All of the cross references has separate numbers for each of the different color varieties (except McKee doesn't mention the $10 no tint because he never saw it). The reference number in this book is for the 'no tint' variation. The 'no tint' doesn't have a protector, and is brown throughout. The rarity number is an overall number (if you add up all the notes for each denomination). This is not an ideal solution, and in the future there will be break downs for each color. The 'no tint' variety is the least common tint found and has been seen as a remainder. Its most commonly found grade is at/around VG. A more thorough examination of this bank is in order.

Omaha – The Brownville Bank & Land Company

Fate: Fraudulent Bank
Date: 1857

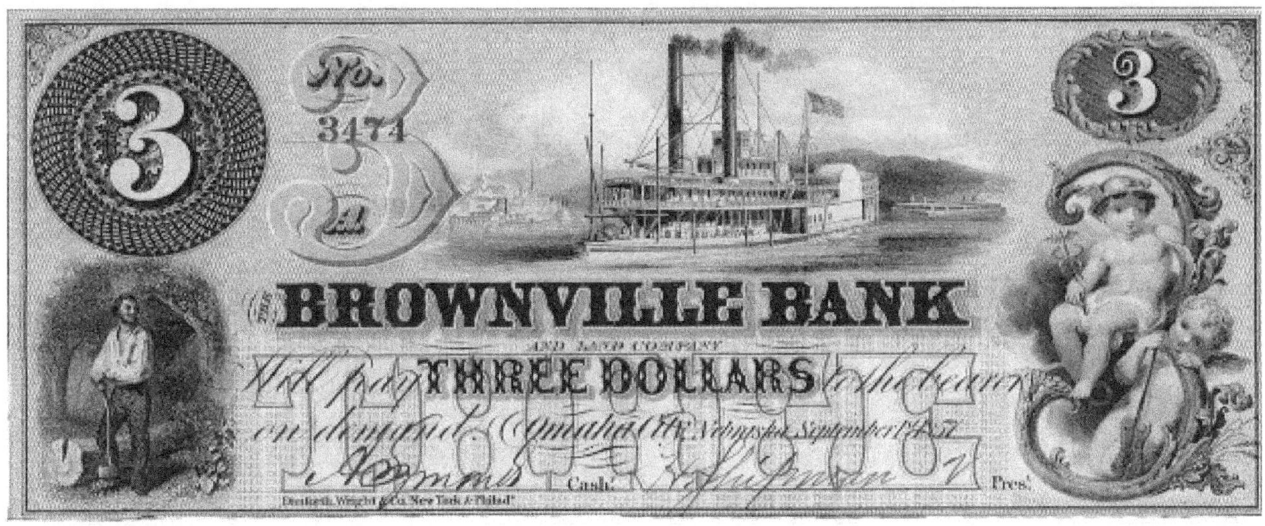

Owen Number	Denomination	Plate Position(s)	Basic Info.	Cross Refs.	Rarity
16-1	$3	A-B	Protector: Large THREE in Tint Imprint: Danford, Wright & Co.	Haxby: 50G2 Walton: 13 McKee: 5	R.4

	VG	XF	AU	UNC
No Tint	$275	-	-	-
Green Tint	$100	-	$600	$850
Yellow Tint	$150	$450	-	-
Brown Tint	$100	$450	-	$900
Red-Brown Tint	$150	-	-	-

Jim McKee Collection

Owen Number	Denomination	Plate Position(s)	Basic Info.	Cross Refs.	Rarity
16-2	$5	A-B	Protector: Large FIVE in Tint Imprint: Danford, Wright & Co.	Haxby: 50G4 Walton: 14 McKee: 10	R.4

	VF	XF	AU	UNC
No Tint	$350	-	-	-
Green Tinit	$100	-	$400	$800
Yellow Tint	$300	-	-	-
Brown Tint	$100	-	$400	$900
Red-Brown Tint	$250	-	-	-

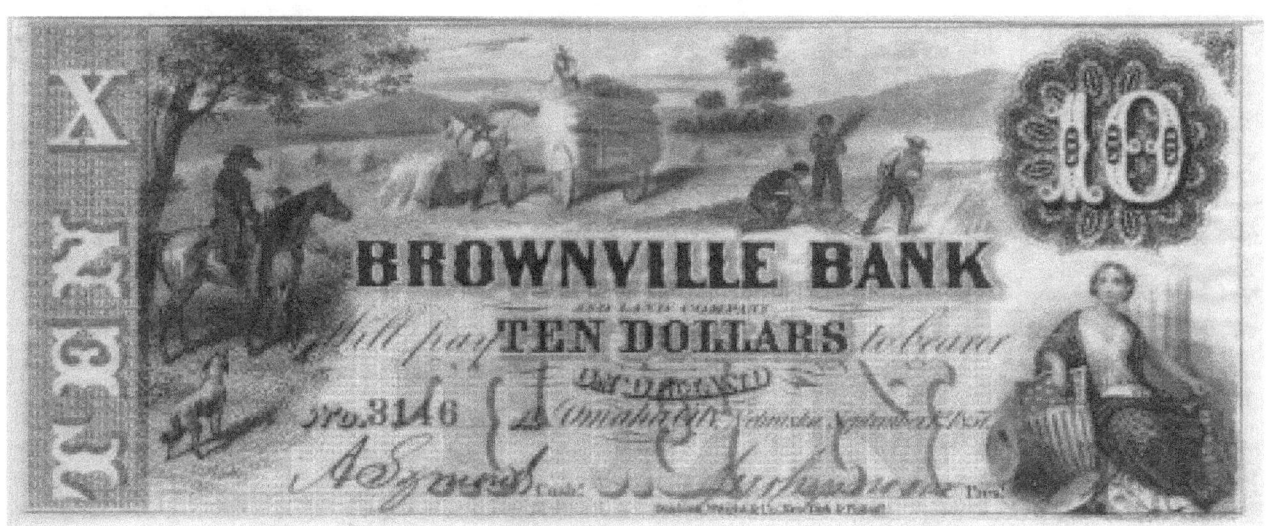

Owen Number	Denomination	Plate Position(s)	Basic Info.	Cross Refs.	Rarity
16-3	$10	A	Protector: Large TEN in Tint Imprint: Danford, Wright & Co.	Haxby: 50G6 Walton: 15 McKee: N/A	R.5

	VG	XF	AU	UNC
No Tint	$175	-	-	-
Green Tint	$175	-	$550	$800
Yellow Tint	$225	-	$550	-
Brown Tint	$200	$400	$800	$1000
Red-Brown Tint	$225	$425	-	-

Images Courtesy of Heritage Auctions.

Owen Number	Denomination	Plate Position(s)	Basic Info.	Cross Refs.	Rarity
16-4	$3-$5-$5-$10	A-B	Protector: Large VALUE in Tint	Haxby: 50GX1-X2	R.4
			Imprint: Danford, Wright & Co.	Walton: N/A	
				McKee: N/A	

	VF	XF	AU	UNC
No Tint	-	-	-	-
Green Tint	-	$1550	-	$1800
Yellow Tint	-	-	-	-
Brown Tint	-	$1400	-	$1800
Red-Brown Tint	-	-	-	-

The City of Omaha

The notes for the City of Omaha were not actually a bank issue. They were issued to obtain funds for the building of the Territorial Capitol. The United States Congress appropriated $50,000 for the building of the Capitol but this was not enough to complete the job. The city of Omaha did not have the additional funds to complete the building, so they issued notes for the remainder needed, much as the Federal Government does today.

The Omaha City scrip was never redeemed. It was issued during the Panic of 1857. On December 14, 1857, the council voted to have a bond issue to retire the scrip. An election was held on December 26, 1857 and the bond issue passed; but since the City of Omaha had a poor credit rating, bond dealers were not interested, and the bonds were never sold.

An auction of City owned lots was held with the provision that these lots could be paid for with City scrip. The lots sold for unheard of prices as the people who owned the notes felt more secure with the land than with the notes. These notes were printed by Wellstood, Hay & Whiting in sheets of four notes with the denominations of $1, $1, $3, and $5. The notes were included because they were issued in 1857, which was during the "wildcat" time span.

These dates appear on the City of Omaha notes: August 20, 1857; October 1, 1857; November 15, 1857; and December 1, 1857. All signed notes have Jesse Lowes (Mayor) and H.C. Anderson (Recorder) on them. Unsigned notes (remainders) are scarce and command a premium.

Omaha – The City of Omaha

Fate: Never Redeemed
Date: 1857

Image Courtesy of Heritage Auctions.

Owen Number	Denomination	Plate Position(s)	Basic Info.	Cross Refs.	Rarity
17-1	$1	A-B	Protector: Large ONE in Red Imprint: Wellstood, Hay & Whiting	Haxby: N/A Walton: 1 McKee: 1	R.1

	VF	XF	AU	UNC
Issued	$50	-	$100	$150
Remainder	$125	-	-	-

Image Courtesy of Heritage Auctions.

Owen Number	Denomination	Plate Position(s)	Basic Info.	Cross Refs.	Rarity
17-2	$3	A	Protector: Large 3 in Red Imprint: Wellstood, Hay & Whiting	Haxby: N/A Walton: 2 McKee: 2	R.1

	VF	XF	AU	UNC
Issued	$50	-	$100	$180
Remainder	-	$100	$200	-

Owen Number	Denomination	Plate Position(s)	Basic Info.	Cross Refs.	Rarity
17-3	$5	A	Protector: Large 5 in Red Imprint: Wellstood, Hay & Whiting	Haxby: N/A Walton: 2 McKee: 2	R.1

	VF	XF	AU	UNC
Issued	$100	$150	$200	$300
Remainder	-	-	-	-

Image Courtesy of Heritage Auctions.

Owen Number	Denomination	Plate Position(s)	Basic Info.	Cross Refs.	Rarity
17-4	$1-$1-$3-$5	A-B	Protector: Large VALUE in Red	Haxby: N/A	R.3
				Walton: N/A	
			Imprint: Wellstood, Hay & Whiting	McKee: N/A	

	VF	XF	AU	UNC
Sheet	-	$600	-	$1200

The Nebraska Land and Banking Company

No records have been found on this bank as to its officers, location, etc. These notes were also printed by Danforth, Wright & Co., with the statement that they were payable on demand at Omaha City. These notes are known in denominations of $1 and $2.

On May 25, 1858, Governor W.A. Richardson wrote a letter to James C. Chapman, District Attorney, First District, N.T. He requested that Mr. Chapman file information against the following banks which had no territorial charters: Saratoga Banking Co.; Omaha City Bank & Land Co.; Nebraska Bank & Land Co.; Pacific Bank & Land Co.; Nebraska Exchange Bank & Land Co.; Brownville Bank & Land Co.; and Omaha & Chicago Bank.

Governor Richardson asked that these banks be closed because "they are not authorized by law, and because they have omitted to redeem and pay their notes when presented for payment, and for such other and further cause as may be found to exist."

No records and no notes have been found for the Nebraska Bank and Land Co., so we assume that Governor Richardson was referring to the Nebraska Land and Banking Company. All signed notes of the Nebraska Land and Banking Company that have been reported bear the signatures of W.T. Finch as president and Wm. McConthe as cashier.

Here is an interesting thought: there may be notes that we have yet to see. Namely from the Saratoga Banking Co., Pacific Bank and Land Co., and the Nebraska Exchange Bank and Land Co.

Currently there is only one known proof sheet (the one that was sold in 1990 through Christie's and then again in April 2012 through Heritage). However, it is not known if that sheet was removed from its PMG holder and cut into singles. As a single proof $1 with plate position 'B' was sold through Stack's Bowers' 2012 November auction.

Omaha – The Nebraska Land and Banking Company

Fate: Disappeared/Failed
Date: 1850s

Image Courtesy of Heritage Auctions.

Owen Number	Denomination	Plate Position(s)	Basic Info.	Cross Refs.	Rarity
18-1	$1	A-C	Protector: Large ONE in Red	Haxby: 60G2a	R.7
				Walton: 1	
			Imprint: Danforth, Wright & Co.	McKee: 1	

	About Good	G	VG	UNC
Issued	$100	-	-	-
Remainder	-	-	$600	-
Proof*	-	-	-	$1,550

*Three were sold in the 1990 Christie's sale, without a red protector. Plate position 'B' sold for $3,300 in the Stack's 2012 Baltimore auction. The price listed is for the 'A' plate which sold in Stack's 2015 Baltimore auction.

Jim McKee Collection

Owen Number	Denomination	Plate Position(s)	Basic Info.	Cross Refs.	Rarity
18-2	$2	A	Protector: Large 2 in Red Imprint: Danforth, Wright & Co.	Haxby: 60G4a Walton: 2 McKee: 2	R.7

	G	VG	XF	UNC
Issued	-	$1000	-	-
Remainder	-	-	-	-
Proof	-	-	-	-

Image Courtesy of Heritage Auctions.

Owen Number	Denomination	Plate Position(s)	Basic Info.	Cross Refs.	Rarity
18-3	$1-$1-$1-$2	A-C	Protector: None	Haxby: N/A	R.7
			Imprint: Danforth, Wright & Co.	Walton: N/A	
				McKee: N/A	

	G	VG	XF	UNC
Proof Sheet	-	-	-	$3,500

*Only one sheet was offered during the Christie's sale of 1990; which is now housed in a PMG64 holder and last sold through Heritage in 2012.

The Omaha and Chicago Bank

The Omaha and Chicago Bank requested a charter from the Third Territorial Legislature but the request was denied. A bill was introduced in the Fourth Session of the Legislature "to prevent the improper issue of the Omaha and Chicago Bank". They issued notes but these notes were redeemed when presented and are very rare today.

The manager of this bank was H.B. Sackett and the cashier was J.V. Schell. The bank was located at 12th and Farnam Streets in the building that had been the home of the Western Exchange Fire and Marine Insurance Company.

The notes of this bank were printed by the American Bank Note Company in sheets of four notes, with the denominations of $1, $2, $5 and $10. These notes had RED protectors. All of these notes are rare and hardly come to public auction. A proof $2 and a proof $5 printed by Bald, Cousland & Co., are known, but these notes were never printed for circulation purposes. These BCC notes can be found with and without the RED protectors in single form or in uncut pairs. Christie's sold 12 sheets in 5 different lots in the large ABNC sale of 1990. Likewise, GREEN protector proofs of $1, $2, $5 and $10 are also known. Some third party graders would call the notes with green protectors Progressive Proofs.

Circulating notes would have had stamped serial numbers.

In 1976 collaboration between the American Bank Note Co. and the International Silver Co. produced a series called the Historic American Currency set. This set included a proprietary proof (from original plates) of the $5 note which was originally printed by Bald, Cousland & Co. Along with this proof came a 5 troy ounce replica of the engraved proof with matching serial numbers. The notes were housed in attractive packaging and came with a booklet detailing the program. On the back of the proof reads "COPY: An authentic reproduction from the original plates (1976)".

Omaha – The Omaha and Chicago Bank

Fate: Disappeared/Redeemed
Date: 1861-62

Image Courtesy of Heritage Auctions.

Owen Number	Denomination	Plate Position(s)	Basic Info.	Cross Refs.	Rarity
19-1	$1	A	Protector: Large ONE in Green Imprint: American Bank Note Co.	Haxby: 65G4a Walton: 1 McKee: 1	R.7

	VF	XF	AU	UNC
Issued (Red)	-	-	-	-
Green Proof	-	-	-	$350

Image Courtesy of Heritage Auctions.

Owen Number	Denomination	Plate Position(s)	Basic Info.	Cross Refs.	Rarity
19-2	$2	A	Protector: Large TWO in Green Imprint: American Bank Note Co.	Haxby: N/A Walton: 2 McKee: N/A	R.7

	VF	XF	AU	UNC
Issued (Red)	-	-	-	-
Green Proof	-	-	-	$460

Image Courtesy of Heritage Auctions.

Owen Number	Denomination	Plate Position(s)	Basic Info.	Cross Refs.	Rarity
19-3	$2	A	Protector: None	Haxby: 65G6	R.7
			Imprint: Bald, Cousland & Co.	Walton: 5	
				McKee: 2	

	VF	XF	AU	UNC
No Procrotor Proof	-	-	-	-
Red Protector Proof	-	-	-	-

Image Courtesy of Heritage Auctions.

Owen Number	Denomination	Plate Position(s)	Basic Info.	Cross Refs.	Rarity
19-4	$5	A	Protector: Large FIVE in Green Imprint: American Bank Note Co.	Haxby: 65G8 Walton: 3 McKee: N/A	R.7

	VF	XF	AU	UNC
Issued (Red)	-	-	-	-
Green Proof	-	$200	-	$700

Jim McKee Collection

Owen Number	Denomination	Plate Position(s)	Basic Info.	Cross Refs.	Rarity
19-5	$5	A	Protector: None	Haxby: N/A	R.7
			Imprint: Bald, Cousland & Co.	Walton: 6	
				McKee: 3	

	VF	XF	AU	UNC
No Procector Proof	-	-	-	-
Red Protector Proof	-	-	-	-

Image Courtesy of Heritage Auctions.

Owen Number	Denomination	Plate Position(s)	Basic Info.	Cross Refs.	Rarity
19-6	$10	A	Protector: Large TEN in Green Imprint: American Bank Note Co.	Haxby: 65G10 Walton: 4 McKee: N/A	R.7

	VF	XF	AU	UNC
Issued (Red)	-	-	-	-
Green Proof	-	-	-	$1000

Owen Number	Denomination	Plate Position(s)	Basic Info.	Cross Refs.	Rarity
19-7	$2/$5*	A	Protector: None	Haxby: N/A	R.1
			Imprint: Bald, Cousland & Co.	Walton: N/A	
				McKee: N/A	

	VF	XF	AU	UNC
Propriretary Proof	-	-	-	$25

*This intaglio printed note was made in 1976 by International Silver Company and American Bank Note Company measuring 8.5" x 4.25" Note is hardly sold by itself, often bought because of the silver note that accompanies it.

Image Courtesy of Heritage Auctions.

Owen Number	Denomination	Plate Position(s)	Basic Info.	Cross Refs.	Rarity
19-8	$2-$5	A	Protector: None	Haxby: N/A	R.6
			Imprint: Bald, Cousland & Co.	Walton: N/A	
				McKee: N/A	

	VF	XF	AU	UNC
Proof Pair	-	-	-	$750

Image Courtesy of Heritage Auctions.

Owen Number	Denomination	Plate Position(s)	Basic Info.	Cross Refs.	Rarity
19-9	$1-$2-$5-$10	A	Protector: Large VALUE in Green Imprint: American Bank Note Co.	Haxby: N/A Walton: N/A McKee: N/A	R.7

	VF	XF	AU	UNC
Proof Sheet	-	-	-	$1000

The Omaha City Bank and Land Company

The Omaha City Bank and Land Co. is another bank that issued notes without the benefit of a charter. They redeemed their notes as presented and signed notes of this bank are very scarce today.

The signed notes bear the signatures of F. Davidson, president, or C.W. Aylseworth, vice president, and R.C. Spain as the cashier. These notes were printed by the American Bank Note Co. – Jocelyn, Draper, Welsch & Co., in sheets of four notes with denominations of $1, $1, $2, and $5.

This bank would regularly publish an ad in the *Omaha City Times* from January 1858 to January 1859. It read "Omaha City Bank & Land Co. This bank is regularly organized and open for business in the banking house formerly occupied by Samuel E. Rogers on Douglas St. F. Davidson Pres't. R.C. Spain Cashier"

All notes have red lathework.

One proof sheet was sold during the Christie's sale of 1990 (Elizabeth 7112) lot 884 and sold for $950.00. It's my assumption that this sheet was unique. However, it appears that the sheet has been cut down into singles. As seen from the 2011 Chicago ANA where a $1, $2 and a $5 did not sell. Time will tell if a) the only proof sheet was cut down or 2) another proof sheet comes to light.

Omaha – The Omaha City Bank and Land Company

Fate: Failed
Date: 1858-59

Owen Number	Denomination	Plate Position(s)	Basic Info.	Cross Refs.	Rarity
20-1	$1	A-B	Protector: Large ONE in Red Imprint: Baldwin, Bald & Cousland	Haxby: 70G2a Walton: 1 McKee: 1	R.3

	VF	XF	AU	UNC
Issued	-	$150	-	-
Remainder	$100	$150	$200	$300
Proof	-	-	-	-

Owen Number	Denomination	Plate Position(s)	Basic Info.	Cross Refs.	Rarity
20-2	$2	A	Protector: Large TWO in Red Imprint: Baldwin, Bald & Cousland	Haxby: 70G4a Walton: 2 McKee: 2	R.4

	VF	XF	AU	UNC
Issued	-	-	$200	-
Remainder	$60	-	-	$400
Proof	-	-	-	$1000

Owen Number	Denomination	Plate Position(s)	Basic Info.	Cross Refs.	Rarity
20-3	$5	A	Protector: Large FIVE in Red Imprint: Baldwin, Bald & Cousland	Haxby: 70G6a Walton: 3 McKee: 3	R.5

	VF	XF	AU	UNC
Issued	$100	-	-	-
Remainder	-	-	$300	-
Proof	-	-	-	-

This note has been seen altered to Utica City Bank - Utica, NY and City Bank of Bath - Bath, ME.

Image Courtesy of Heritage Auctions.

Owen Number	Denomination	Plate Position(s)	Basic Info.	Cross Refs.	Rarity
20-4	$1-$1-$2-$5	A-B	Protector: Large VALUE in Red Imprint: Baldwin, Bald & Cousland	Haxby: 70X1 Walton: N/A McKee: N/A	R.7
		VF	XF	AU	UNC
Sheet		-	-	-	$1200

The Western Exchange and Land Company

This is another bank that issued notes with no record of a charter being requested. Denomination of $1, $5 and $10 are known, but this bank must have redeemed its notes as presented, as these notes are extremely rare. These notes were printed by Wellstood, Hay & Whiting.

This is the only Nebraska obsolete notes that bear coinage on them. There isn't a lot of information on this back, and this bank doesn't have anything to do with the more common Western Exchange Fire & Marine Insurance (Owen 22). Because this bank didn't apply for a charter, and the latter did.

Without ever seeing an uncut sheet we can still make an educated guess as to what the sheet structure was. Looking at the plate positions we can infer that there were two sheets produced 1) $1-$1-$1-$2 and 2) $5-$5-$10-$10. Or the second sheet could have been $5-$10-$10-$10. This would make more sense as it would mirror the smaller denomination sheet. More research will have to be done or we can wait until a few more $5 or $10 come to market to see if we can find a 'B' plate or a 'C' plate on a $10.

Omaha – The Western Exchange and Land Company

Fate: Dissolved
Date: 1857-58

Image Courtesy of Heritage Auctions.

Owen Number	Denomination	Plate Position(s)	Basic Info.	Cross Refs.	Rarity
21-1	$1	A-C	Protector: Large ONE in Red Imprint: Wellstood, Hay & Whiting	Haxby: 75G2a Walton: 1 McKee: 1	R.7

	AG	F	VF	XF
Issued	$350	$1,500	$2,000	-

Image Courtesy of Heritage Auctions.

Owen Number	Denomination	Plate Position(s)	Basic Info.	Cross Refs.	Rarity
21-2	$2	A	Protector: Large TWO in Red	Haxby: 75G4a	R.7
				Walton: N/A	
			Imprint: Wellstood, Hay & Whiting	McKee: N/A	

	AG	F	VF	XF
Issued	$100	$1,000	$2,000	-

Jim McKee Collection

Owen Number	Denomination	Plate Position(s)	Basic Info.	Cross Refs.	Rarity
21-3	$5	A	Protector: Large FIVE in Red Imprint: Wellstood, Hay & Whiting	Haxby: 75G6a Walton: 2 McKee: N/A	R.7

	G	F	VF	XF
Issued	$100	$1,000	$2,000	-

Image Courtesy of Heritage Auctions.

Owen Number	Denomination	Plate Position(s)	Basic Info.	Cross Refs.	Rarity
21-4	$10	A-B	Protector: Large TEN in Red Imprint: Wellstood, Hay & Whiting	Haxby: 75G8a Walton: 3 McKee: N/A	R.7

	VG	F	VF	XF
Issued	$400	$950	$1,200	-

The Western Exchange Fire and Marine Insurance Company

The Western Exchange Fire and Marine Insurance Co. received its charter from the Legislature on March 16, 1855. This was during the first session of the Legislature and this was the only "bank" to receive a charter at this session. The charter was a permit to receive deposits and issue certificates therefor, so their notes were certificates of deposit.

The incorporators were: R.W. Lathnam, William Kempton, James S. Izard, J. McNeale, W.E. Moore, Thomas H. Benton Jr., and associates. LeRoy Tuttle was the cashier of this bank and A.U. Wyman was the teller. The signatures on the signed notes of the Omaha issue are Tuttle (Secretary), and Benton (President). The signature titles change on the $10 and $20 to Cashier and President, but the signers remain the same. This bank went bust on September 23, 1857. The bank was owned by Greene, Weare, and Benton of Cedar Rapids, Iowa, who had other banks in Iowa.

More of the notes of this bank were in circulation in Iowa than of any other bank. After the failure of this bank in September 1857, Mr. Olof Johnson of Galva, Illinois, purchased the charter from Mr. Benton for a reported price of $9,500. Mr. Johnson was an officer and member of the Bishop Hill Colony.

A new issue of notes was ordered with the following added: "deposited by Bishop Hill Colony," and with a printed date of November 2, 1857. The Bishop Hill issue was an Illinois issue and had nothing to do with the earlier Nebraska issue. Mr. Johnson continued to redeem the earlier issue along with his own issue until the money ran out and the bank when bust again. The Bishop Hill issues of notes were signed by Tuttle (Secretary) and Johnson (President).

Few of the Bishop Hill issues (22-7 to 22-10) were put in circulation, and crisp notes as well as uncut sheets of this issue are quite common today. All issues of notes of this bank were printed by Danforth, Wright & Co. The sheets were of the four note variety with the denominations of $1, $2, $3 and $5. $10 and $20 (22-1 to 22-6) notes of the Omaha issue are known but the sheet lay out is not known for these denominations.

All of the Omaha issues of the notes of this bank are scarce with the $10 and $20 denomination being a little bit tougher to find. These Omaha issues had hand signed serial numbers and date. The Bishop Hill issues used stamped serial numbering and the date is engraved.

The Bank of Nebraska and the Western Exchange Fire and Marine Insurance Company were the only two institutions that operated with a charter, although some of the non-chartered institutions redeemed their issues remarkably well.

One proof sheet was sold at the 1990 Chritie's sale. That note is now housed in a PCGS 63 apparent holder. Several $10-$20 proof pairs were also sold at the same Christie's sale.

This remains one of the more readily available banks for collectors to obtain - Even in Superb Gem Uncirculated (68) - Although this is only for the Bishop Hill notes with zero signatures which were more-than-likely cut from a sheet with a skilled hand. Expect to pay a premium for notes graded 67 and higher of around 30% of UNC prices.

The Bishop Hill sheet is easily found with zero signatures (R.1), somewhat easy to find with one signature (R.2), and with a little patience the issued sheets come up about every other month or so (R.3).

A rarity change from Walton's last edition: He gave the $10 and the $20 a R.7; they are now R.6 and R.5 respectively. I have observed 6 $10's, and eleven $20's. As more time passes expect to see more of this scarce variety.

These notes were still in circulation well after the bank failed according to "Banker's Almanac 1861" this bank had its original $50,000 in capital and still had an undisclosed amount of notes in circulation. Including Bank of De Soto (Owen 7), Bank of Florence (Owen 11), Platte Valley Bank (Owen 13), Bank of Nebraska (Owen 15), and Bank of Tekama (Owen 22) there were a total of $600,000 in circulation and the banks retained $100,000 in specie in 1861.

Omaha – The Western Exchange Fire & Marine Insurance Co.

Fate: Failed, Sold, and Failed Again
Date: 1855-57

Owen Number	Denomination	Plate Position(s)	Basic Info.	Cross Refs.	Rarity
22-1	$1	A	Protector: Large ONE in Red Imprint: Danforth, Wright & Co.	Haxby: 80 Walton: 1 McKee: 1	R.4

	VF	XF	AU	UNC
Issued: 1856	$45	-	$175	-
Proof*	-	-	-	-

*Without red protector

Owen Number	Denomination	Plate Position(s)	Basic Info.	Cross Refs.	Rarity
22-2	$2	A	Protector: Large TWO in Red Imprint: Danforth, Wright & Co.	Haxby: 80 Walton: 2 McKee: 3	R.4

		VF	XF	AU	UNC
Issued: 1856		$55	-	$175	-
Proof*		-	-	-	$500

*Without red protector

Owen Number	Denomination	Plate Position(s)	Basic Info.	Cross Refs.	Rarity
22-3	$3	A	Protector: Large THREE in Red Imprint: Danforth, Wright & Co.	Haxby: 80 Walton: 3 McKee: 5	R.4

	VF	XF	AU	UNC
Issued: 1856	-	-	$175	-

Owen Number	Denomination	Plate Position(s)	Basic Info.	Cross Refs.	Rarity
22-4	$5	A	Protector: Large FIVE in Red Imprint: Danforth, Wright & Co.	Haxby: 80 Walton: 4 McKee: 7	R.4

	VF	XF	AU	UNC
Issued: 1856	$65	$100	$175	-

Owen Number	Denomination	Plate Position(s)	Basic Info.	Cross Refs.	Rarity
22-5	$10	A	Protector: Large TEN in Red Imprint: Danforth, Wright & Co.	Haxby: 80 Walton: 5 McKee: 9	R.6

	F	VF	XF	AU
Issued: 1856	$100	-	-	$750

Image Courtesy of Heritage Auctions.

Owen Number	Denomination	Plate Position(s)	Basic Info.	Cross Refs.	Rarity
22-6	$20	A	Protector: Large XX in Red Imprint: Danforth, Wright & Co.	Haxby: 80 Walton: 6 McKee: 10	R.5

	F	VF	XF	AU
Issued: 1856	$200	$350	-	$850

Owen Number	Denomination	Plate Position(s)	Basic Info.	Cross Refs.	Rarity
22-7	$1	A	Protector: Large ONE in Red Imprint: Danforth, Wright & Co.	Haxby: 80 Walton: 7 McKee: 2	R.1

	VF	XF	AU	UNC
Issued: 1857	-	-	-	$115
1 Signature	-	-	$60	$100
0 Signatures	-	-	$85	$115

Owen Number	Denomination	Plate Position(s)	Basic Info.	Cross Refs.	Rarity
22-8	$2	A	Protector: Large TWO in Red Imprint: Danforth, Wright & Co.	Haxby: 80 Walton: 8 McKee: 4	R.1

	VF	XF	AU	UNC
Issued: 1857	-	-	$85	$115
1 Signature	-	-	-	$100
0 Signatures	-	-	$100	$125

Owen Number	Denomination	Plate Position(s)	Basic Info.	Cross Refs.	Rarity
22-9	$3	A	Protector: Large THREE in Red Imprint: Danforth, Wright & Co.	Haxby: 80 Walton: 9 McKee: 6	R.1

	VF	XF	AU	UNC
Issued: 1857	-	-	$100	-
1 Signature	-	-	-	$100
0 Signatures	-	-	$100	$125

Owen Number	Denomination	Plate Position(s)	Basic Info.	Cross Refs.	Rarity
22-10	$5	A	Protector: Large FIVE in Red Imprint: Danforth, Wright & Co.	Haxby: 80 Walton: 10 McKee: 8	R.1

	VF	XF	AU	UNC
Issued: 1857	-	-	-	-
1 Signature	$65	-	$100	-
0 Signatures	-	-	$100	$125

Images Courtesy of Heritage Auctions.

Owen Number	Denomination	Plate Position(s)	Basic Info.	Cross Refs.	Rarity
22-11*	$1-$2	A	Protector: Large VALUE in Red Imprint: Danforth, Wright & Co.	Haxby: 80 Walton: N/A McKee: N/A	R.7

	VF	XF	AU	UNC
Without Protector**	-	-	-	$2500
With Red Protector**	-	-	-	$3000

*These are both proofs, one with the red protector and one without.
**5 with red protectors and 1 without were sold during the 1990 Christie's sale.

Image Courtesy of Heritage Auctions.

Owen Number	Denomination	Plate Position(s)	Basic Info.	Cross Refs.	Rarity
22-12	$1-$2-$3-$5	A	Protector: Large VALUE in Red	Haxby: 80	R.1
				Walton: N/A	
			Imprint: Danforth, Wright & Co.	McKee: N/A	

	VF	XF	AU	UNC
Proof (1856)	-	-	-	$2700
Issued: 1857	-	-	$300	-
1 Signature	-	-	$225	$275
0 Signatures	-	-	$180	$230

Plattsmouth

The first mention of Plattsmouth was in 1854, and at that time it was known as just "The Barracks" which was named after a trading post. Three people co-owned the trading post - Sam Martin, owner of the Platteville Ferry (in nearby Mills County, Iowa), Wheatley Mickelwait (ferryman), and Colonel Joseph Longworthy Sharp (a Glenwood, Iowa attorney and politician). On March 15, 1855 Plattsmouth (named for the city resting on the mouth of the Platte River) was incorporated. A city government was elected on December 29, 1856 when Wheatley Mickelwait was appointed Mayor, Enos Williams, W.M. Slaughter and Jacob Vallery were elected Aldermen.

The council first met to conduct business on January 29, 1857 and their first ordinance, approved by Mayor Mickelwait on March 2, 1857, was to levy a tax of one-half of 1 per cent on all taxable property within the city limits. The money collected would be for the improvement of the streets, alleys, and steam boat landings. The following scrip notes may have something to do with that ordinance.

Plattsmouth hold the county seat for Cass County. By 1860 there were around 474 people living in Plattsmouth. As of the 2010 census 6,502 people now live in the city.

It is unknown if these scrip notes were ever used or issued. Each denomination used a different printer's name. However, both notes come from the same print shop. Robert W. Furnas founding member of the Nebraska Advertiser (though he would be given full control of the paper from the remaining shares from Dr John McPherson) and Chester S. Langdon were editor and publisher respectively through the end of 1859.

Plattsmouth – The City of Plattsmouth

Fate: Unknown
Date: 1858

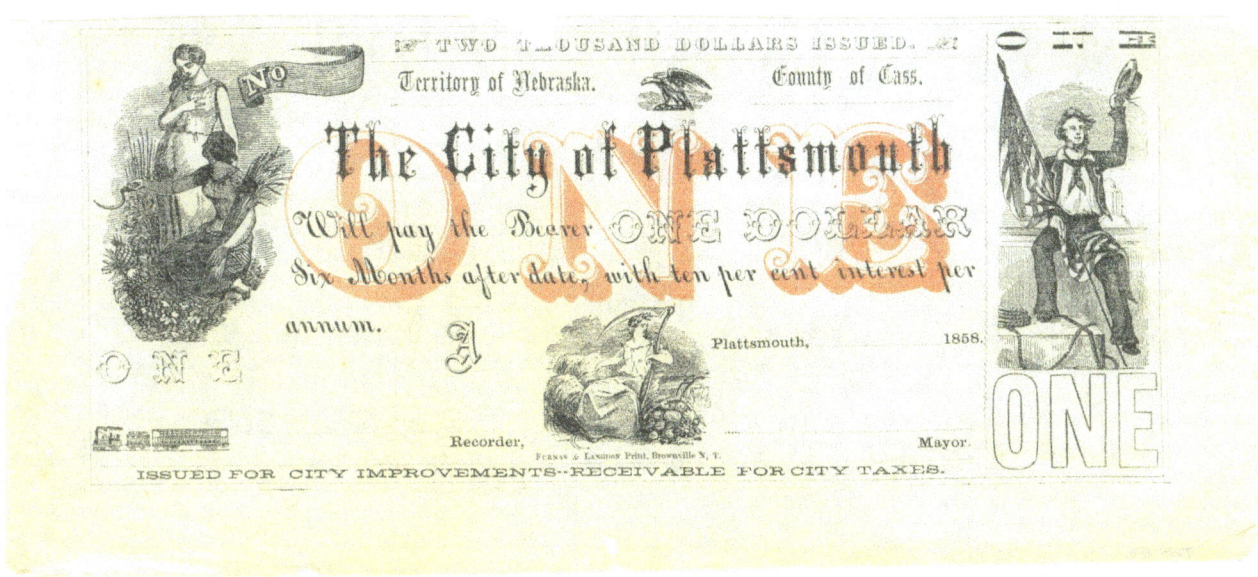

NHSH Collection

Owen Number	Denomination	Plate Position(s)	Basic Info.	Cross Refs.	Rarity
23-1	$1	A	Protector: Large ONE in Red Imprint: Furnas & Langdon Print, Brownville NT	Haxby: N/A Walton: 1 McKee: 1	R.7

	VF	XF	AU	UNC
Issued	-	-	-	-

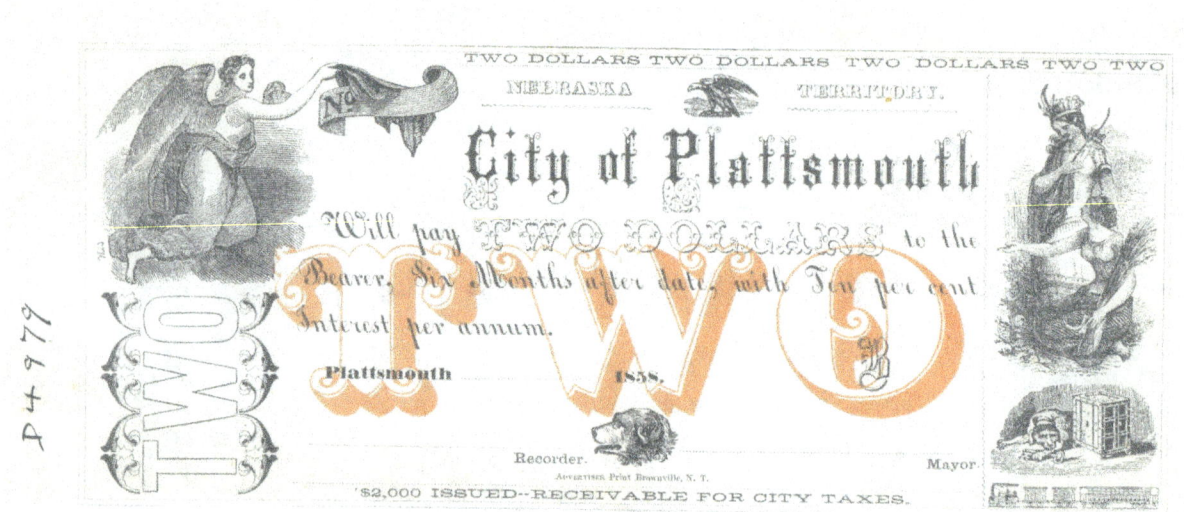

NHSH Collection

Owen Number	Denomination	Plate Position(s)	Basic Info.	Cross Refs.	Rarity
23-2	$2	A-B	Protector: Large TWO in Red Imprint: Advertiser Print Brownville NT	Haxby: N/A Walton: 2 McKee: 2	R.7

	VF	XF	AU	UNC
Issued	-	-	-	-

Tekamah

The Centennial "Gazetteer" of the United States, printed in 1874, had very little to say about Tekamah. This brief description was all they had to say about this interesting town of the early territorial days. "Tekamah, postal village and the county seat of Burt County, Nebraska, 46 miles north of Omaha. One Newspaper."

The town of Tekamah only had one bank, known as "The Bank of Tekama". Note the spelling of "Tekama" on the notes. The town of Tekamah has always been spelled with an "h" on the end. No one has been able to explain the reason for this discrepancy. The bank act, as passes, used the name without the "h".

The Bank of Tekama received a 25 year charter from the Legislature on February 12, 1857. This charter was vetoed by Governor Mark W. Izard, but was passed over his veto.

The Incorporators were listed as follows: S.L. Campbell (president), F.W. Akin (cashier), T.M. Puett, W.C. Brewster, B.B. Northrop, W.A. Moore, W.N. Byers, G.W. Chilcott, Luther Newton, F.R. Wright, L.P. Baman, Judson R. Heyde, and J.F. Wilson.

This bank was supposed to have issued $99,000, most of which was never redeemed, which gave it the name of the worst of the "Wildcats" or obsolete banks. These notes are listed as Rarity 3 (51-100). If the reports of the amount unredeemed are true, an undiscovered hoard of thousands of notes must be hiding somewhere.

When a bank failed, all of the newspapers of the day wrote editorials about the event. The informational masterpieces of two of these publications are listed below.

The "Nebraska Advertiser" (Brownville, Nebraska) announced on May 27, 1858, that the bank had failed. "Messers, Carson and Lushbaugh, bankers of this city, had returned to them on Tuesday last, an amount they had sent to Omaha for redemption, the bank failing to redeem it. At Omaha, the bills are said not to be worth 2 ½ cents on the dollar. A gentleman just down from above, informs us that the sheriff of Burt County had seized upon the bank and safe, which he opened, but found nothing but Tekama bills."

The "Nebraska City News", on May 29, 1858, gave the following information on the Tekama Bank.

"Maj. James D. White has just returned from the den of the ferocious animal, and reports him to be one of the greatest in size, and most ferocious of any of the species that have been discovered in Nebraska; not excepting the Fontenelle or Nemaha. The Major says that he made a diligent search for the animal for several days, and finally found him in an obscure corner of land in the lower edge of Burt County, saw him in all his native wildness."

The "Nebraska City News", on July 31, 1858 added this further information on the Bank of Tekama:

"If there was a single cat in Nebraska more wild, more feline, in every characteristic than another, it was the Bank of Tekama. It was a bas fraud, an open swindle, a lie and a cheat from the beginning unto the end."

Other newspapers of the day had their stories to tell, but the few listed will demonstrate the general idea of the type of articles to be found.

It was common for newspaper writers to talk about the bank as if it were an actual wildcat. The term wildcat may have originated from a bank in Michigan who had vignettes of wildcats on them. This bank ultimately failed. While others suggest that it was a common colloquial term used in reference as a risky business endeavor. Currently, the term wildcat isn't used as much as obsolete, and some may argue that the term broken bank note is incorrect as some banks never broke (or failed).

Tobe Height was the assistant cashier, who managed the bank in Tekamah. He was described by Major White as "a rather good looking specimen of the genus homo."

A.T. Andreas, in his History of the State of Nebraska, written in 1882, gives the best account of early Tekamah.

"Tekamah, the county seat, is located in the southeastern part of Burt County. The first claim made on the present site of Tekamah was by B.R. Folsom, W.N. Byers, J.W. Patterson, H.C. Purple, John Young, Jerry Folsom, Mr. Maynard William T. Raymond, and Mr. White, in the name of the Nebraska Stock Company, on October 7, 1854. This claim was an area of four miles square. The first permanent settlement in Tekamah was made on April 19, 1855, by B.R. Folsom, Z.B. Wilder, John B. Folsom, Niles R. Folsom, William F. Goodwill (who remained permanently), and a few others."

Note that W.N. Byers is the only one of the incorporators of the Bank of Tekama that actually lived in Tekamah.

"Tekamah was incorporated as a city very early in its history, on March 14, 1855, and became the county seat at the same time. Olney Harrington was made Postmaster in 1855. Miles Chillcot opened the first store in 1856. The first school was taught by J.R. Conkling in 1857 and the first sermon was preached on Sunday,

November 5, 1854, by a Methodist minister. The first newspaper was the Burt County Pilot, established in 1871, by J.W. Lambert, which moved to Blair in 1874. Tekamah has one graded school, with four teachers, and one ward school. The principal school building is a fine two-story frame, costing $5,000, and located in a pleasant park of nearly two acres. Tekamah is on the Chicago, St. Paul, Minneapolis, and Omaha Railroad, which affords fine shopping facilities. In 1880, the United States census gave it a population of 776. It is now (1882) estimated at 1,000. The town contains various business establishments, and some of the enterprising businessmen have recently erected fine brick homes. It has good hotel accommodations, the last hotel being a fine two-story brick erected in 1880."

According to the 2010 census there are 1,736 people living in Tekamah and is still the county seat of Burt County.

The note illustrations of the Bank of Tekama are all dated September 1, 1857, which is the date found on most, if not all of these notes. These notes were printed by Baldwin, Bald, and Cousland in sheets of four notes $1A, $1B, $2A, and $5A - where the letters correspond to the plate position. The one dollar note illustrated has the St. Louis overprint. Presumable the notes so stamped were payable in St. Louis.

Even in 1861 Bank of Tekama notes were still in circulation. According to "Banker's Almanac 1861" this bank had $100,000 in capital and still had an undisclosed amount of notes in circulation. Including Bank of De Soto (Owen 7), Bank of Florence (Owen 11), Platte Valley Bank (Owen 13), Bank of Nebraska (Owen 15), Bank of Tekama, and Western Marine Insurance Co (Owen 22) there were a total of $600,000 in circulation and the banks retained $100,000 in specie in 1861.

Tekamah – The Bank of Tekama

Fate: Went broke
Date: 1857-58

Owen Number	Denomination	Plate Position(s)	Basic Info.	Cross Refs.	Rarity
24-1	$1	A-B	Protector: Large ONE in Red Imprint: Baldwin, Bald & Cousland	Haxby: 85G2a Walton: 1 McKee: 1	R.3

	VF	XF	AU	UNC
Issued	$65	$100	$200	-
"St. Louis" Stamp	$90	$100	-	-
Proof	-	-	-	$600

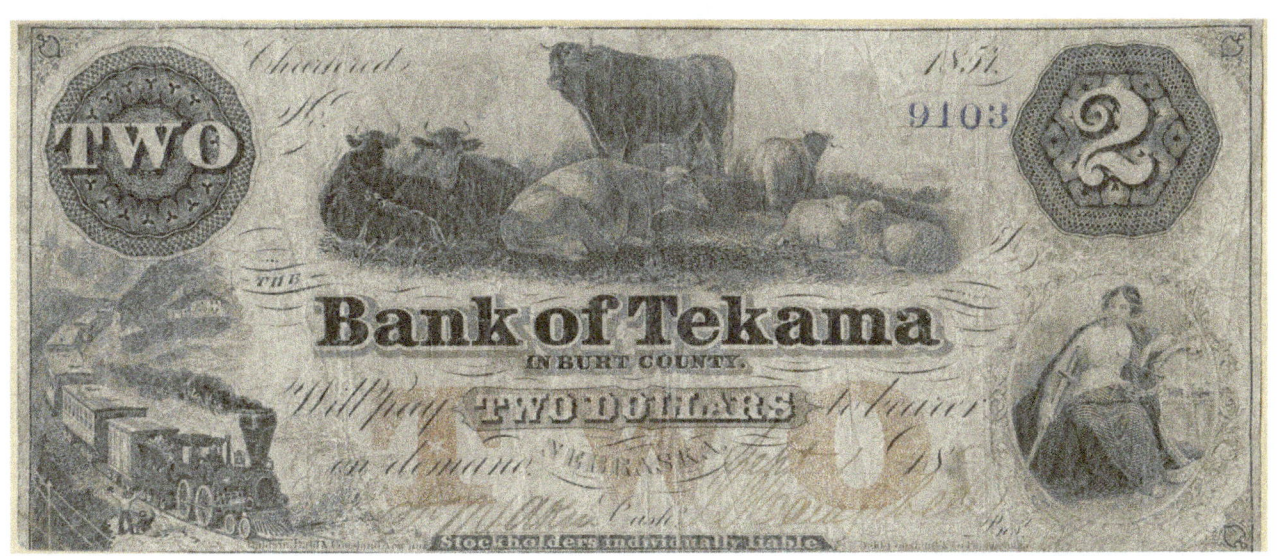

Byron Reed Collection

Owen Number	Denomination	Plate Position(s)	Basic Info.	Cross Refs.	Rarity
24-2	$2	A	Protector: Large TWO in Red	Haxby: 85G4a	R.3
				Walton: 2	
			Imprint: Baldwin, Bald & Cousland	McKee: 2	

	VF	XF	AU	UNC
Issued	$65	-	$200	-
"St. Louis" Stamp	-	$80	-	-
Proof	-	-	-	-

Byron Reed Collection

Owen Number	Denomination	Plate Position(s)	Basic Info.	Cross Refs.	Rarity
24-3	$5	A	Protector: Large FIVE in Red Imprint: Baldwin, Bald & Cousland	Haxby: 85G6a Walton: 3 McKee: 3	R.3

	VF	XF	AU	UNC
Issued	$75	-	$200	-
"St. Louis" Stamp	$85	-	-	-
Proof	-	-	-	-

Image Courtesy of Heritage Auctions.

Owen Number	Denomination	Plate Position(s)	Basic Info.	Cross Refs.	Rarity
24-4	$1-$2	A-B	Protector: None	Haxby: N/A	R.7
			Imprint: Baldwin, Bald & Cousland	Walton: N/A	
				McKee: N/A	

	VF	XF	AU	UNC
Proof Pair*	-	-	-	$700

*It is this researchers estimation that this was cut from a sheet (which would explain the lone $1 - expect to find a lone $5 in the future). Another clue is that the plate position of the $1 is 'B' while the $2 is 'A' - exactly like the full sheet.

Image Courtesy of Heritage Auctions.

Owen Number	Denomination	Plate Position(s)	Basic Info.	Cross Refs.	Rarity
24-5	$1-$1-$2-$5	A-B	Protector: None	Haxby: N/A	R.7
			Imprint: Baldwin, Bald & Cousland	Walton: N/A	
				McKee: N/A	

	VF	XF	AU	UNC
Proof Sheet*	-	-	$500	$1000

*Four sheets were sold during Christie's 1990 ABN auction. All were described with tears and/or tape repairs.

STRONG BUYERS OF NEBRASKA NATIONAL BANK AND OBSOLETE NOTES

Call Bjorn-308-222-0340 or 308-455-1550

info@kearneycoincenter.com - kearneycoincenter.com

2006 Central Ave Kearney, Ne 68847

To order this book/ebook:

1) www.NebraskaPaperMoney.com
2) JayRecher@yahoo.com
3) www.facebook.com/NebraskaPaperMoney
4) www.JayRecher.com/Store
5) www.amazon.com

Wholesale options are available

Brown Brothers

We Buy & Sell
Currency Dealer
www.thenumismaticshop.com

(251) 943-3122

Appendix A

The Brownville Bank & Land Co. (Owen-16) Color Tints*:

No Tint:

Green Tint:

Yellow Tint:

Brown Tint:

Red-Brown Tint:

*Colors can change over time do to various reasons - enviroment, storage, circulation, etc.

Appendix B

List of Private Bankers* (Circa 1861-63):

City	County	Private Banker	NY Correspondent
Brownville	Nemaha County	H.M. Atkinson	Lewis B. Brown & Co.
Brownville	Nemaha County	J.L. Carson	J.W. Carson & Co. (Phil.)
Brownville	Nemaha County	L. Hoadly	Lewis B. Brown & Co.
Nebraska City	Otoe County	McCann & Metcalf	Hoffman & Co./Colegate & Hoffman
Nebraska City	Otoe County	John H. Maxon	Woodruff & Co./The Park Bank
Nebraska City	Otoe County	James Sweet & Co.	American Exchange Bank
Nebraska City	Otoe County	J.A. Ware	Drexel Read & Co.
Omaha City	Douglas County	Millard Barrows & Co.	Son Gilman & Co.
Omaha City	Douglas County	J. Clark & Brother	Son Gilman & Co.
Omaha City	Douglas County	Kountze Brothers	The Park Bank/Chemical Bank
Omaha City	Douglas County	Smith & Parmelee	Broadway Bank
Virginia City	Douglas County	Paxton & Thornburgh	None

*This list is not complete, and ever growing. This researcher assumes all private bankers had some form of paper money (either checks, certificates of deposit, or otherwise).

Bibliography

Auction Companies:

Heritage Auctions (www.ha.com)
Lyn Knight Auctions (www.lynknight.com)
Stack's Bowers Galleries (www.stacksbowers.com)

Andreas, A. T. (1975). *History of the State of Nebraska*. 1882. Reprint, with index. Evansville, IN: Unigraphic Inc.

Barrett, Jay A. (1898). *Nebraska and the Nation*. J.H. Miller.

Burr, G.L, Buck, O.O., & Stough, D.P (1921). *History of Hamilton and Clay Counties, Nebraska: Volume 1*. S.J. Clarke Publishing Co.

Carey, Fred. (1929). *Romance of Omaha*. <http://www.historicomaha.com/romance.htm>.

Fitzpatrick, Lillian L. (1960). *Nebraska Place Names (New Edition)*. Univ. of Nebraska Press.

Johnson, Harrison (1880). *Johnson's History of Nebraska*. H. Gibson.

McKee, James L. (1970). *The Wildcat Bank Notes, Scrip and Currencies of Nebraska Prior to 1900*.

Morton, J.S., Watkins, A., & Miller, G.L (1913). *Illustrated History of Nebraska: A History of Nebraska from the Earliest Explorations of the Trans-Mississippi Region, Volume 1*. J. North.

Office of the Bankers Magazine (1861). *Banker's Almanac and Register and Legal Directory*. J. Smith Homans, Jr. Page 40, 58.

Office of the Bankers Magazine (1863). *Banker's Almanac and Register and Legal Directory*. J. Smith Homans, Jr. Page 23, 37.

Olson, James C. (1966). *History of Nebraska*. Lincoln, NE: Univ. of Nebraska Press,

Owen, Leonard M. (1984). *Territorial Baning in Nebraska*. Central States Numismatic Society.

Richardson, Charles Howard (2011). *Pioneer Settlement of Nebraska Territory: Based on the Original Survey 1855-56*. Traffard Publishing.

Savage, James W. and Bell, John T. (1894). *History of the city of Omaha, Nebraska*. New York, Chicago, Munsell & Company.

Sheldon, Addison E. (2008). *History and Stories of Nebraska*. Reprint. Kessinger Publishing, LLC.

Simmons, Jerold (1976). *La Belle Vue: Studies in the History of Belluve, Nebraska*. Mayor's Advisory Commitee.

Sorenson, Alfred (2009). *The Early History of Omaha*. Reprint. Bibliographical Center for Research.

Walton, Gerome (1978). *A History of Nebraska Banking and Paper Money*. Centennial.